KU-284-098

FOURTH LEADERS

Printed in Great Britain

FOURTH LEADERS

FROM

THE TIMES

1952

A selection from the past twelve months

LONDON

THE TIMES PUBLISHING COMPANY LIMITED

PRINTING HOUSE SQUARE

CONTENTS

THE FAR-FETCHED FLEA

"I feel a real and deep humility in having this flea called by my name." In these curiously moving words MR. CHARLES POMERANTZ, once a dress designer in New York, is reported to have acknowledged the gift, from the American Pest Control Association, of a large model or statuette of *Stivalius pomerantzi.* The flea itself was actually discovered, we are told, "on a rat on top of a mountain in the Philippines" by a MAJOR TRUB. The scene conjured up is a dramatic one. The lonely peak, bathed in the Technicolor splendour of a tropic dawn; the intrepid major, his hand shaking ever so slightly with emotion as he pops *Stivalius* into his killing-bottle; the old rat watching with a lump in his throat as his little *protégé* is borne away to achieve fame in New York, where his name will be, if not in lights, at least in italics.

In the scientific world it is not done for a discoverer to name whatever he has discovered after himself, though a learned body may bestow this honour on him. If A. N. Other comes across a new species of rhinoceros he does not ostentatiously dub it *otheri*, though he may, so to speak, keep the thing in the family by calling it *fifiae* after the woman he adores. A more normal practice is to give it the name either of a distinguished rhinoceros-fancier or else of someone who, though having no particular connexion with pachyderms, is generally regarded as a benefactor of mankind. All sorts of odd beasts, one rather imagines, are called *stalini* in Russia. On this occasion the former practice was followed; MR. POMERANTZ has for fifteen years made distinguished contributions to the study of human parasites.

Different people, luckily, have different ambitions, otherwise the world would be in an even worse mess than it is ; and no one will grudge MR. POMERANTZ the honour which he has so richly earned. Precious few of us will live to see our surname, shunted rather brusquely into the genitive, tacked on to either animal, vegetable, or mineral. We would almost all jump at the chance of being immortalized, if it could possibly be arranged, by having something called after us. *Pêche Melba*, Wellington boots, *boeuf Stroganoff*, Plimsoll line, Becher's Brook, Hobson's choice, Skinner's Horse, Avenue Foch, Richardson's skua, Hadrian's Wall, Charley's Aunt—but already the list (in which none of us figures) has wandered away from the orderly realm of science and the dark immensities of the undiscovered. The question of how keen any of us would be on having a flea named after him is academic. One hopes that we should all accept the honour with humility, tinged no doubt with a secret pride and a still more secret sense of gratitude that it was not the other way round.

HOT OR COLD

The " cold war " is a good phrase for a bad thing, but, like many metaphors, it has its dangers for journalists and politicians. " Is the right hon. gentleman aware that tens of millions of people are looking to him to raise the icy temperature of the cold war ? " asked a member of Parliament the other day. One sees what he meant, but it is evidence of the confusion surrounding the whole business that at least one newspaper quoted him as saying " reduce the icy temperature." Clearly the first thing to decide is whether we want the cold war to be colder or hotter. At first sight it seems obvious enough. Only a callous war-monger could want the thing any colder than it is already, so that the aim should surely be to raise the temperature. On the other hand, if the phrase means anything at all—as one rapidly begins to doubt—it is meant to imply that a cold war, in which nations bombard each other with Notes, is preferable to a hot war, in which they use what are politely called " conventional weapons." But if a cold war is better than a hot war, then it is also better than a tepid war or a lukewarm war. In that case the wisest thing is to leave the temperature alone.

It is possible, of course, that the man who first thought of the phrase was thinking of the ordinary Fahrenheit thermometer. According to this theory international relations become unpleasantly warm if they rise above 80 degrees but unpleasantly cold if they fall below freezing point. This would simplify matters for we could then reasonably ask statesmen to keep cool and to preserve their *sang-froid* while scolding them if they showed themselves cold towards any proposals for peace. Those who failed would no doubt get a hot reception or a cold reception according to the nature of their fault. If the temperature rose above 100 degrees we should be in danger of a hot war; below zero a state of cold war would be declared automatically.

This solution would certainly enable politicians to talk of raising and lowering the temperature without any inconsistency. It would imply that there existed a kind of temperate zone, rather like the climate of England, where nations could conduct their affairs in a decent and normal manner. Even so there is much to be said for sticking to well-tried metaphors about storms. Storms at least offer some variety. Nations may face them, ride them out, weather them, or even turn their backs to them. There are useful calms which come after or before. Cold wars, however, are singularly intractable. They cannot be thawed or frozen; they cannot be fought and won. Having taken their temperatures night and morning there is really nothing left to do but to stop them —and that, of course, is more easily said than done.

AFTER TAKING

Modern advertisements often depict the human race in an unflattering light. Ladies and gentlemen are shown ("Before Taking") to be suffering from a variety of disabilities and blemishes of which the cumulative effect is often to make them the victims of a form of social ostracism. Wallflowers, if not pariahs, they are seen gazing enviously at the sort of harem which has automatically collected round the man who has conquered his dandruff or at the squad of suitors drawn, as by a magnet, to the girl who uses Glam. Since in the case of many of the products advertised we ourselves are still in the "Before Taking" stage, these advertisements tend to have a slightly lowering effect on our morale. It is true that the indifference, only qualified by revulsion, with which society regards their protagonists is rather more marked than the polite incuriosity with which it regards us; but it would on the whole be nicer if the advertisers could, without any sacrifice of integrity, show us glimpses of a world less chronically haunted by minor personal tragedies, a world where the emphasis was on perfection rather than on vulnerability.

This half-conscious preference is splendidly catered for by the travel agencies, the shipping companies, the air lines, and all the other firms whose object it is to persuade us to embark on the hazards and uncertainties of a journey. In their advertisements all is sweetness and light. The photographer has cleverly caught the atmosphere of relaxed *bonhomie* which pervades the interior of the air-liner or the cocktail bar of the ocean greyhound. Faultlessly dressed, distinguished without being overpoweringly so, the passengers are clearly filled with a kind of inner happiness. See what delicious viands they are eating in the restaurant car. Observe the solicitude with which the attendants minister to their needs. Nobody looks untidy or torpid or ill-tempered. All are transfigured by a strange mixture of serenity and complacency.

The curious thing is that, when we do travel, we never seem to meet these people. We cannot even claim to be one of them ourselves. When we try to loll gracefully back, as we have so often seen them doing, in our seat in the aeroplane, our clothes wrinkle unbecomingly and very soon, most likely, we fall asleep with our mouth wide open and several of our waistcoat buttons undone in a posture which, if we were photographed, would give a very poor impression of the delights of air travel. In the restaurant car there does not seem to exist between us and the harassed attendant who shovels boiled potatoes on to our plate quite the same gracious, almost feudal relationship which we remember from the advertisements; and if these led us to suppose that our partner in the deck quoits championship was virtually certain to be a young lady of startling physical beauty they led us, we very frequently discover, to suppose wrong. Somewhere, perhaps, they exist, these glossy, radiant voyagers who beam at us from the windows of the travel agencies as though both exalted and stupefied by the elixir of travel. It is strange that, however copiously we swig down that elixir ourselves, we never find ourselves travelling in their company.

A NEW HOLMES MYSTERY

Amateur detectives have for years been on the trail of Holmes and Watson as keenly as that ever diverse pair used to be on that of Moriarty, and from the REVEREND SIDNEY AUSTERBERRY, rector of St. Alkmund's Church, Shrewsbury, there comes an appeal which should be greatly to their taste. In a visitors' book he has found the signature of ARTHUR CONAN DOYLE and under it the breathtaking words, " I have thought out a Sherlock Holmes story here." This is indeed the stuff to give the troops of the Baker Street Irregulars, who confine their investigations to microscopic scrutiny of the text of the stories. It must be confessed that some research into, for instance, the tangled skein of Watson's matrimonial affairs has, on occasions, seemed a trifle self-conscious and heavy-handed, but this is something novel, and the only trouble with the clue to the story CONAN DOYLE thought out is that it seems as barren as the bowler-hat in the case of the Blue Carbuncle seemed to the dull and undiscerning eye of Watson.

The Church, to start with, certainly argues clergymen. Holmes had a wide circle of clients, ranging from *incognito* kings, dukes, and prime ministers down through the social scale to the infatuated Miss Sutherland and the indignant employee of the Red Headed League, but his contacts with the Church were few and unfortunate. There was the unfrocked old scoundrel who performed the forced marriage the solitary cyclist was too late to prevent and, if he can count, the deplorable Peters, who so nearly got away with the murder of Lady Frances Carfax. In general, however, Holmes might, in his conversation with the worried captain of the Cambridge Rugby XV, have added the clergy to amateur sportsmen as among those with whom he seldom had to deal. If there is not much help to be gained from clergymen, neither is there from the church or the churchyard, for the Holmes stories are singularly free from the rattle of skeletons, the smell of the charnel house, of midnight and the open grave, although there is, to be sure, the corpse of the too intelligent butler entombed alive beside the Stuart crown to consider and the ghoulish behaviour of the desperate racehorse owner who had to win the Derby. Yet there is one story—and that the best—which does suggest that it might have been thought on in a churchyard; the sense of vigil in it is strong. It may be that as CONAN DOYLE pondered among the quiet of the graves a vision came to him of another quiet, the quiet of a night when two men waited about a bed for a shutter to open and the band, the speckled band, to creep down the dummy bell-rope about its deadly business. At any rate that is one theory, and certain it is that there will soon be as many theories as there are lovers of Holmes, some of whom may be ready to put their favourite for the story conceived in a churchyard on a level with the Elegy itself.

DEAR DOG

Evidence that dogs can read has, hitherto, rested shakily on the word of the owner of a shaggy dog who tried to take him into a cinema on the plea that he had so enjoyed the book of the film. Now, a letter, produced at the Assizes, has incurred the censure of the court because it was so offensive that it ought not to have been written even to a dog. This proof that the law recognizes the possibility of a dog receiving a letter would have been more complete had it included the reasons why a wider licence of discourtesy is permissible in canine than in human correspondence. An ardent Cambridge man has been heard to say that he would not even send his dog to Oxford, but even he might object to the animal's being made the target of poison pens.

Temptation to write to one's own dog from his youth upwards might no doubt be strong. Looking at him in his basket, deep in the sleep that comes to dogs, just and unjust, and recalling the sins of omission and commission with which the day has been plentifully bestrewed, the least eloquent of owners could find just the right note to strike. This, he would write, is the age of the common dog, and if you are to do yourself—and me—credit in it, you must begin by learning to be a common puppy and this does not mean doing all the mischief that your father did at your time of life. Remember, he was brought up when privilege and inequality flourished. There were, then, thoroughbreds and mongrels. Small wonder that, inhibited and frustrated as he was, he chewed slippers, chased kittens, and preferred running riot to walking to heel. The common dog has too keen a nose for social values to lower himself like that. The only catch is that the puppy will come upon reports of dog shows and find that democracy, alas, is still round the corner and that prizes are still going to the pedigreed.

Progress may alter this, but it will have far to go if it is to evolve dogs who are not the most dreadful nuisances when they expect letters by the post. That, once they have had one by a single post, they will demand a regular stream, is as sure as that bones are bones. The advent of the postman will cease to be a cause of offence and an excuse for angry barking. Letters will be picked up as they fall on to the mat and retrieved with an appealing look, asking " Are there any for me ? " Wives will take their husbands anxiously aside and murmur, " There is nothing for Bob this morning and you know how disappointed he will be." Trouble in private houses will be nothing to that in kennels. Imagine a letter from an old bitch of the Horn to a dog hound of the Upland Downland commiserating with him on his pack having mislaid their fox on three successive days and asking him whether the present of a brace of hares would cheer up his young entry. The more closely the scope of this development in communication is considered, the trickier it seems and the greater the chances that the courts—which are apparently ready for it—will have their hands full.

SMOKE AND GROW FAT

A last defence against smoking has been attacked by the speaker at the British Association who said that thin men are the smallest smokers. This, like so many scientific observations, runs contrary to the unreliable evidence casually collected in the course of everyday life. Unblushing sybarites, who have never made the forlorn attempt to stop smoking, are often confronted, as they fill their pipes or open their cigarette cases, by the envious eyes of a friend in the throes of voluntary martyrdom. It is, he says, so many days—in hardened cases, so many months—since he smoked. If he is developing into a liar —and the chances are that he is, for abstinence of this sort tends to breed pride and other compensating vices— he adds that he has lost all or nearly all his taste for tobacco. His longing eyes betray him, but the smoker, who, being well contented, can afford to be tactful, congratulates him and asks if self-denial has produced any incidental effects. Invariably, the answer is given in stones and pounds. Since the fast began the sweet ration, hitherto spurned, has proved insufficient and second helpings have become the order of every meal.

At the back of the mind of the martyr has always, hitherto, been the thought that he had an honourable way out of his misery. Lighting up again brazenly in front of the friends whom he had been impressing with his powers of self-control, he could say that the renewal of the tobacco habit had been made necessary for reasons of health. He had been getting too fat. Now it seems that, if he had only stuck to his toffee and his rice puddings and left cigarettes alone, he could have got himself permanently below the welter class and, perhaps, among the feathers. Stubbing out the final cigarette must, in future, be to burn one's boats with a vengeance—to cross, irretrievably, to the Non-Smokers' bank of the social Rubicon. Better never to have ventured on the ferry trip than to paddle back to humiliation and an extra two stone. Best of all, like HAECKEL, never to have tasted the delights of smoking and to be able, proudly, to claim " I have had no experience of tobacco, except in its botanical aspects."

Philosophy of that practical sort will not be enough for some recruits to abstention and they may seek to drown—or at least to dilute—their cravings for tobacco in drink. Here, again, science has them by the throat. Drinking, the same speaker at Edinburgh warns them, sends the tell-tale arrow on the weighing machine farther round on its clockwise course no less surely than does smoking. But, they may argue in desperation, if we keep off tobacco, we shall reap the reward of a sensitive palate and be able to enjoy fine wine and—so little of that can we afford—it will not put on more than an ounce or so to our weights ; our ancestors, who were connoisseurs of vintage, despised tobacco—at any rate until the port had circulated. History, coming to the aid of science, banishes that pipe dream. The DUKE of WELLINGTON, in an order to his officers, expressed concern that the use of pipes, cigars, or cheroots had become prevalent and went on to denounce the " species of intoxication occasioned by the fumes of tobacco " as, undoubtedly, being the cause of drinking and tippling in those who acquire the habit. Smoking, then, leads to drinking and both lead to loss of figure. The laugh is with the lean—only they dare not indulge in it, for fear of getting fat.

THE VIRTUE OF CONSTANCY

Excessive cinema-going, the moralists agree, is reprehensible. It leads, some would say, to gum-chewing and the gallows, to vagueness of mind and vulgarity of speech, softening the brain when it does not sharpen wayward wits into illicit ways. The young, in the view of all except the young, should be protected against it. With older people it is perhaps another matter. A bad habit long continued has a way of becoming a good one, or at any rate of winning acceptance as not so bad after all. Sanctified by sentiment and long usage, the vices and shortcomings of youth—the smoking and the billiards—become the peccadilloes of later life, and even its gentle virtues. And as a virtue, surely, we must regard the record of that Eltham old lady who at a local cinema the other day was presented with a bedside lamp because she has attended twice a week since the cinema was opened, twenty-nine years ago.

To go twice a week to " the pictures " without regard to what the pictures were might be condemned in a younger person as revealing, to put it kindly, a certain lack of discrimination and initiative. Even an older person, after a year or two of the habit, might be warned that he had got into a rut. But to stay the course for nearly thirty years to the age of eighty-one, and always to go to the same cinema as this faithful patron has done, must silence criticism. The compulsion of habit is elevated into the virtue of constancy. " It was the first picture house I ever visited," the old lady said, and she has never allowed herself to be lured away from it by the tempting propaganda of other palaces. " I like a good laugh and a good cry," she said, and who could have a better right to either? "Full harde it is to fynde a woman stedfast," but here is one, and if sometimes "the one eye wepe" and "the other do the contrary," it only shows how true to life the films at Eltham are.

GO WEST, OLD MAN

In those countries that are collectively known as western, democratic, or simply free, authority has recently become increasingly perturbed by the Communist exploitation of youth. This anxiety is no doubt a tribute to the watchfulness and forethought of our rulers, even though it sometimes seems a little exaggerated, but it is clear that they have been less successful in thinking of counter-measures. It is usually assumed, for instance, that the proper reply to a Communist demonstration of youth is a non-Communist demonstration of youth. The ill-effects of the World Festival of Youth at Berlin, it was urged, are best countered by the international youth camp on the Rhine, by the world jamboree of boy scouts, and by the World Assembly of Youth now meeting at Cornell University. Altogether admirable though these gatherings are, in their own right, no one has yet suggested the obvious solution. The proper answer to a festival of youth is not another festival of youth but a festival of age.

It is frequently urged that the future belongs to youth. Those who do so apparently forget that by the time the future arrives the youth will no longer be young. The present, which, after all, is what matters in politics, invariably belongs to the aged and often to the very aged indeed. Youth, in fact, is an absurdly transient condition lasting—so far as voters are concerned—a mere five or six years. Clearly it is not worth the consideration of any serious politician. A little thought will quickly show, moreover, that, while no one is going to be young, nearly everybody—granted reasonable luck and an adequate supply of penicillin—is going to be old. Conversely, everyone ceases to be young but no one ceases to be old until he ceases to be anything at all.

The festival of age should clearly be held at some place like Bournemouth or Torquay where there are adequate supplies of doctors and bath-chairs. As the trains stream into the station, carrying delegations from all respectable countries, they would be met by ancient Britons carrying banners with the slogan " Old Age for Peace ! " on one side and " Peace for Old Age ! " on the other. Clearly no age limit would be necessary and it would be a matter for the organizing committee to decide whether or not to impose a youth limit instead. Fortunately—and it is yet another advantage of the scheme—the aged are singularly free from prejudice in this matter, and while genuine boys and girls are inclined to look critically at pot-bellied gentlemen in shorts leading youth parades, no one will object if a few children join the grand march of the aged to the town hall. There the age battalions will join in singing the festival song, which will be something on the lines of

> Grow old along with us;
> The West is bound to win.

What a happy picture it would be! And what a pity that, owing to the chronic preoccupation with youth, we shall never be able to see it.

SOMEONE AT THE DOOR

The notice which hangs on the front door of a house in London, "No papers. No salvage. *Pas d'oignons*," is symptomatic of the strain that can be imposed on householders through the medium of the door-bell. "Not many sounds in life," wrote CHARLES LAMB, "and I include all urban and all rustic sounds, exceed in interest a knock at the door." To-day, misgiving rather than interest is the predominant emotion. It is not that friends and neighbours are any less welcome than they were. It is not even that our relations with inspectors, the deliverers of parcels or the collectors of debts have noticeably deteriorated. It is rather that the army of hawkers, dealers in junk, scrap and bric-à-brac, and the enthusiastic but entirely uncoordinated attempts of youth to turn an honest penny by collecting salvage, seem to have grown or, at any rate, that we seem to be more than ever exposed to their forays.

Those who live in flats may escape this particular ordeal; and other families who have acquired the good services of a Slovene or a Tyrolean, a Florentine or a Basque, are, to some extent, sheltered from it. The rest, and in particular those whose front doors give bravely on to the street, are a prey to every form of itinerant merchant, most of them equipped with all the attributes of modern salesmanship. There are times when they are welcome. The vendor of peat or onions or shoelaces may bring just what we want at the moment; the dealer may even offer to pay money for what has hitherto been worthless clutter in the attic; but such chances are rare. More often these days our mood is

> Tie up the knocker! Say I'm sick, I'm dead.

Less drastic ways may be sought of abating the nuisance. The suspicious occupant of a house who used to answer every summons to his door from an upstairs window, peering first, perhaps, from behind a handy curtain, tended to be considered an eccentric who had something to hide or some reason to shun his callers. To-day, solid, guiltless citizens, who should be able to look the whole world in the face, are being forced in self-defence to adopt the same method of what is nowadays called, to MR. CHURCHILL's indignation, screening. The notice hung outside—whether it takes the form of the long-established warning "No hawkers or circulars" or follows the more individualist example quoted above—tries to tackle the problem at its roots. That, in practice, it will have no deterrent effect at all is only too likely.

A COLLECTOR'S ROUNDS

Nearly everybody collects something, but scarcely anybody can understand the attraction of what somebody else collects. Utterly puzzling to the unimaginative are the herds of small boys who to-day haunt railway stations, each armed with his little note-book. In that book he appears to inscribe some eagerly sought figures, but the question whether he is scanning engines or carriages or trucks entirely defeats the stodgy traveller lolling in a state of lamentable boredom in the corner seat. Sherlock Holmes collected murderers—"A pin, a cork, and a card," he exclaimed of that villainous entomologist, Stapleton, "and we add him to the Baker Street collection!" The list of these various enthusiasts is an unending one, and to it must now be added a gentleman of New York who is justifiably regarded in his native country as "Golf Course Collecting Champion."

It appears that in the forty years during which he has been hunting this entrancing quarry, this prodigy has already played on 2,985 courses, in every state in the United States, every province in Canada, and in nine countries in South and Central America. That is a tremendous record. Yet in spite of his name, which flaunts the glory of a Scottish origin, MR. KENNEDY has never played in the original home of golf. Now, in putting an end to this reproach, he will rapidly accomplish a little matter of fourteen more courses, easy enough, perhaps, in Scotland, where an energetic pilgrim can often play on three courses a day. This will bring his score to 2,999, and then he will play his 3,000th round on the Old Course at St. Andrews.

Metaphorical trumpets should sound and drums be beaten for such a conquering hero. Everybody would normally wish that on this great occasion he may play the game of his lifetime, but it must be remembered that St. Andrews possesses certain classical bunkers and that no one who goes there in the true spirit of pilgrimage would desire wholly to avoid them. “ I wish him no ill,” remarked a spectator of one of the players in a match, “ but I wish he was in a bunker.” So, in the friendliest way, we may wish that, if only out of piety and politeness, MR. KENNEDY may pay a formal visit at least to Strath and Hell and the Principal's Nose. And if he could contrive to putt—as many a good man has done before him—into that trappy little Road bunker at the seventeenth, he would be made free of St. Andrews once and for all.

LOOKING BACK

Yesterday a small gathering at Boscobel celebrated the escape of CHARLES II after his defeat at the battle of Worcester. Three days before another small gathering at Worcester remembered with gratitude CROMWELL'S victory over CHARLES—a victory which, MR. ISAAC FOOT claimed, determined the future of this country and the future of the world. Ceremonies such as these are as much a part of the English scene as the pageant at the village fête. The poetry of history, says DR. TREVELYAN, lies in the fact that

> once on this earth, once on this familiar spot of ground, walked other men and women, as actual as we are to-day, thinking their own thoughts, swayed by their own passions, but now all gone, one generation vanishing after another, gone as utterly as we ourselves shall shortly be gone like a ghost at cock-crow.

The pilgrims who have travelled this week to Worcester and Boscobel have sensed the poetry of history. Centenaries—and tercentenaries—ought to be celebrated; they rescue history from the bookshelves, and bring our ancestors back to colourful life—" not mere creatures of fiction and imagination, but warm-blooded realities even as we are."

It is right, too, that the champions of the Royalist and Puritan causes to-day should—with passionate and unfeigned conviction—revive the controversies of the seventeenth century. These are not dead issues; they are a part of us. Our political institutions were not all that was changed by the events of those dramatic twenty years, from 1640 to 1660. We ourselves would be a different people—thinking differently, feeling differently, acting differently—if CROMWELL'S Ironsides had not won their crushing victories at Marston Moor and Naseby, and if

CHARLES had not escaped from Worcester to return nine years later as king. (What a tragedy it might have been if not he but his brother, JAMES II, had been restored to the throne in 1660.) It is right, therefore, that MR. ISAAC FOOT and MR. ARTHUR BRYANT should challenge each other warmly on these issues, but it is no less right that the majority of their fellow-countrymen should keep calm. We have reason to be thankful that the wounds of our own Civil War have long since healed, and that the divisions of 1651 no longer trouble us in 1951.

Both the Puritan Revolution and the Restoration were steps forward in the development of English Parliamentary government. The strength of the British constitution has not been the separation of powers but the " unity of will," to use a phrase of POLLARD, " as expressed by the Crown in Parliament," and in this sense the Restoration was a return to normal. The Tudors' secret of ruling jointly and harmoniously with their Parliaments was forgotten by QUEEN ELIZABETH towards the end of her reign when she formed a " new alliance of Church and Crown against Parliament," and when CHARLES I completed the process the revolt of Parliament was inevitable. The Restoration—not of the King only, but of the King in Parliament—was therefore not a return to the conditions of 1640. Arbitrary rule based on prerogative had been repudiated as certainly as had arbitrary rule by civilian or military juntas, and this was the lasting feature of CROMWELL'S work. If, as DR. TREVELYAN has said, it is important that we became a nation governed by Parliament in the seventeenth century and did not postpone our rebellion against monarchical power as late as did other nations, then both CROMWELL'S victories and the Restoration should be equally remembered.

BACK TO THE GOOD EARTH

The devoted gardener is glad, on the whole, to be back from holiday. His only grievance against his garden is its immobility. His neighbour on the left, whose hobby is golf, finds fulfilment on the seaside links. Even his neighbour on the right, who dotes on the hens, can—and once did—make a crate for them and take them with him for a fortnight on a farm. But you cannot put a garden in the guard's van, and the earnest cultivator must face with what fortitude he can at holiday times a life divorced from his treasured patch. This is never very far from his homing thoughts—as his family has been known to complain—but the daily care of it must be left in the hands of Nature. And she, he often feels, is a shade irresponsible. Her ways are not his ways, nor her green thoughts his thoughts. What exactly she is aiming at he cannot be quite sure, but it does not seem to be the spirit-level lawn, the carefully crocheted border, the disciplined vegetable plot which he has in mind himself. She has a way of choosing the season of his holiday to water the earth to excess, and suffers with complacence such indiscriminate growth that when he gets home again—if his tale may be believed—the house is scarcely visible from the gate.

Yet the holiday is not a total loss. It may, when properly approached, be borne without fretting and turned to useful account. There is time to wade a little way through the lush growth of gardening books. Health and strength are gained for the tasks of autumn. Inspiration is gathered from a visit to a great estate, though its vistas will not suffer transplanting to the visitor's own landed properties. Wrinkles may be won in long, leisurely talks with other exiles of like disposition. And one year the devoted gardener saw something of a field study centre. It was only a call in passing, but he saw a few rarities in a large untidy garden, and met a pleasant tutor who insisted on showing him a minute kind of fungus that was growing in the grass before the house. It took a bit of finding, going on hands and knees, but at last it was found, and exulted over, and the tutor rose stiffly to his feet. " I hope," he said, surveying with affection the unshorn grass around, " I hope they won't make a lawn out of this." That year, when the gardener got home again, the weeds seemed easier to bear.

CONSIDERING

A foreigner would probably be hard put to it to decide by which item in their extensive though disorderly vocabulary the British most surely reveal their national character. The British are in no such difficulty about the foreigner. They recognize, in the word " verboten," a pregnant clue to the Teuton's desire at all costs to be regimented. They know that the Russians constantly say " Nichevo " because they are feckless and have so much to put up with. Though they have never actually heard an inhabitant of the Middle East say " Kismet," they believe the proud fatalism implicit in this disyllable to be typical of the outlook on life shared by all better-class Arabs; and if they have been to China they will tell you dogmatically that " mei yu fa-tse " (meaning, roughly, that it cannot be helped) is the phrase most frequently to be heard among the philosophical Chinese.

What, in Great Britain, is the equivalent of these useful linguistic signposts? What word or phrase, when we utter it, causes our visitors to smile at each other in the knowing, superior, and yet affectionate manner which we adopt when we hear a Latin American say " Mañana "? Exclamations like " By Jove! " or " Well played, sir! " or " I say, how absolutely spiffing! ", though easily recognizable by the foreigner as part of our idiom, do not really tell him much about us. Like " Begorrah! ", " Sapristi! " or " Nom d'un chien! " they are merely bits of local colour which literature has taught him to identify as such. Not in such trappings, picturesque though they are, is to be found the password which will let the stranger past our guard, the sesame which will open the recondite antres of the British character.

If such a thing exists, it may be the word " considering." In these rather unrewarding times it is more often than ever on our lips. " Oh, it wasn't bad," we say, " considering." Considering what? Nobody—luckily—asks us. What on earth do we mean when we say that the weather was quite good, considering? Have we in fact considered the presence, during the period under review, of a depression over the Bay of Biscay? Not on your life. We have considered nothing; no mental activity of the type specified has taken place. There are, it is true, times when the word does cover a sort of unconscious marshalling in the back of our mind of various associated factors. When, for instance, we say, " I thought George made quite a good speech, considering," a close and brutal interrogation would probably reveal that what we meant was " considering (*a*) that George was our fag at school, (*b*) that almost all speeches are boring anyhow, (*c*) that there were only fourteen people present, (*d*) that the rain was making a frightful noise on the roof of the marquee, and (*e*) that George had had a very late night the night before." We did not realize at the time that we meant all these things. We simply used " considering " as we had so often used it before. It is a symptom of laziness, a product of half-baked and sluggish cerebration; yet it implies a certain stolid philosophy, a capacity for tolerance, an acceptance of the fact that things might almost always have been worse than they were. If one word had to be selected as a clue to the British character, this one might not be such a bad choice, considering.

FOR CHILDREN OF ALL AGES

Learned annotation of nursery rhymes might seem, at first sight, to be as odd an exercise as wearing cap and gown when bathing the baby. Even those baleful pedants who blighted SHAKESPEARE for generations of school children by tracing the plays back to unreadable sources might get off with a lighter sentence than is deserved by the commentator who finds a Greek original, complete with accents, for "hey diddle diddle." Pedantry is the unseasonable ostentation of learning, but, in the *magnum opus* that the Oxford University Press has just published on nursery rhymes, scholarship marches gaily and keeps in step with the spirit of its fascinating theme. Even a statistical table, looking like an extract from the Board of Trade Returns, proves, on examination, to be delightful. Nearly one in four of the familiar rhymes is believed, as this table shows, to have been known when SHAKESPEARE was a young man.

Few of the old authors wrote for children and their original wording was often unsuited, by modern standards, for the nursery. All manner of adult echoes can be detected. There are fragments of ballad and folk song, remnants of ancient custom and ritual, and memories of street cry and mummers' play. The only rhymes going back before 1800 which were written for the nursery seem to be rhyming alphabets, verses to go with games and lullabies. Even the riddles were in the first place designed for adult perplexity. IONA and PETER OPIE, the editors of this novel Oxford Dictionary, argue that Stuart and early Hanoverian parents saw nothing unusual in their children hearing strong language and savouring strong drink. So slow was the growth of a special literature in this *genre* that no earlier use of the term "nursery rhyme " can be found than 1824. Still, there were collections before that, and an old name for them, " Mother Goose Songs," still holds the field in America.

When the origin of the favourites is explored, honest scholarship has often to confess itself baffled. Who killed Cock Robin is, for instance, a question that may have been asked at the fall of WALPOLE'S Ministry in 1742 and may have had something to do with the Norse tale of the death of Balder. Jack Spratt may have been a Stuart dwarf and he may have been a Frenchman, known to the peasants of the Bocage who were alleged to sing :—

Jaques Spras
N'aimoit pas le gras,
Sa femme le maigre détestoit;
Ainsi, que ses deux
Rien au monde n'alloit mieux,
Et rien sur la table ne restait.

If this be accepted (as the Oxford editors are too full of fun to do), then the coast is clear for other theorists. Bo-peep becomes MARY QUEEN of SCOTS, Curlylocks CHARLES II, Old Mother Hubbard CARDINAL WOLSEY, and the pussy in " I love little pussy " QUEEN ELIZABETH. It would be nice to have faith in the theory that " Hush-a-bye, baby," the best known lullaby on either side of the Atlantic, was composed by a Pilgrim youth who went over in the Mayflower and who was influenced by the way the Red Indian hung his birch-bark cradle on the branch of the tree. Enthusiasm more tepid is provoked by the suggestion that " baa baa black sheep's " three bags full is a reference to an export tax of 1275. Imagination shrinks from the thought of " Taffy was a Thief " being sung on the first of March on the Welsh border. The charm of this Dictionary is that it glosses the rhymes with so graceful a mixture of scholarship and humour. Too ponderous for childish hands to hold, it is admirable for reading aloud and its pictures can be shared by all eyes. This is as it should be in an art that is first loved before the meaning of words is known.

STOP AND ASK

" Hadn't you better stop," they mildly suggest, " and ask the way ? " The impact of these words upon a motorist is odd, to say the least of it. For some time past he has been uneasily aware that the place-names on the signposts are unfamiliar or anyhow inappropriate, and his mind is haunted by the vision of a turning, now left many miles behind, down which (he strongly suspects) he should have turned, but did not. His car is not a runaway horse, nor is it being hotly pursued by a pack of wolves ; it would be neither difficult nor disadvantageous to arrest its progress for a moment. He is, nevertheless, possessed by a stubborn, insensate reluctance to do so ; and when at last he does pull up he is in a sulky frame of mind.

This is not dissipated by the almost rapturous complacency with which his chosen guide informs him that he is on the wrong road altogether. The best thing he can do, he is told, is to turn round and go back as far as —But no. Wait a minute. The guide, feeling the need of a second opinion, summons a neighbour from the threshold of The Red Lion, " This gentleman," he explains with merry incredulity, " is trying to get to Scribblebury." " Scribblebury ! " exclaims the neighbour, as though scarcely able to believe his ears, " He is on the wrong road altogether." He directs at the motorist a searching scrutiny. " The best thing you can do," he says, " is to turn round and go back—." " That's just what I was telling him," interrupts the guide. " No good going on down this road. It's just taking him farther and farther out of his way." He gives a pleasant laugh.

This intelligence does not come as a surprise to the motorist ; it only confirms suspicions on which, he fully realizes, he should have acted much earlier ; but the manner of its delivery fills him with a sullen, unreasoning resentment. Why should these two oafs regard—and their manner clearly implies that they do regard—a detailed knowledge of the topography of this godforsaken district as an indispensable part of every Briton's intellectual equipment? Has nobody ever missed his way in this part of the world before? Why must the natives treat him as a phenomenon at once *outré*, risible and pathetic? When, indeed often a little before, they have finished redirecting him, he thanks them curtly and moves off with a great grinding of gears to turn his car round. "Don't forget," they cry as he passes them once more, "third left past the crossroads, then take the right fork when you come to a pond. . . ." Their well-meant admonitions die away. "How lucky we were," says the passenger, "to find such nice, helpful men." The motorist grunts.

A FOWLER IN WHITEHALL

SIR ERNEST GOWERS, intrepid as a missionary among cannibals, is, for the second time, pleading with Civil servants to stick to a diet of plain words. He follows up, to-day, his admirable, provocative, and official little book of three years ago with an *A.B.C. of Plain Words* published by the Stationery Office as part of the armament drive alleged to be in full swing in Whitehall against "officialese." All who risk putting words on paper, in print or in letters, will sympathize with Civil servants whose lapses from the simple prose preferred by FOWLER and other pundits are pounced upon with unrelenting glee. The finger of scorn (see "cliché" in the new guide) is pointed often, but without noticeable effect, at the authors of "commercialese." They cheerfully continue to acknowledge esteemed favours received ult. and to beg to inform their correspondents that a reply to hand before even date will oblige. Civil servants, judging by the hopeful interest taken in them by SIR ERNEST GOWERS, are evidently considered to be less hard cases than are their fellow offenders in the City and in newspaper offices. A millennium may be on its way in which committees are just committees and not always "appropriate" ones and in which their members do not blush to report that "most of us thought" instead of booming out that "a majority was of opinion."

Inflation is the main enemy of officialese as a clipped currency is of some popular writing. "Journalese" in its old-fashioned sense of cumbrous synonyms—domiciliary residence for house—has been dead almost as long as GEORGE AUGUSTUS SALA, but arch little colloquialisms and frenzied efforts to keep abreast with up-to-the-minute (and generally American) idioms can make torture out of a paragraph. The skeletons discovered by Sir Ernest Gowers in the files and in-trays of the Civil Service are, it is fair to say, not the only bones that rattle " in this context " (see guide *passim* and see it, again, for the use of Latin tags). Whitehall, as all its many pleasant and civilized inhabitants individually agree and as few of them seem to be able to remember when they write collectively, could go to school with profit, using this A.B.C. as its primer. It would have saved the application " for a general increase in the ceilings " and it will, if it is taken to heart, curb the roving disposition of " deadline," a word which, as Sir Ernest Gowers points out, began life as meaning " a line drawn round a military prison beyond which a prisoner may be shot down " and has, since, carved out for itself a surprisingly versatile civilian career.

A long-felt want would be met if Sir Ernest Gowers had the good fortune to convert a maximum of his own colleagues and to induce them to pay optimum attention to his doctrine. There would be a gratifying reduction in the overall throughput of the Stationery Office and of the official mailbags. A slimming process would be applied to the sentence " The position regarding this matter is that owing to the fact that two claims were made by two claimants of the same name some confusion arose." Weighing itself after treatment by the A.B.C. this would be reduced to " Confusion arose because there were two claimants of the same name." What would happen to some political speeches and leading articles if they were taken through the same exercise is a question that Whitehall may reasonably ask. If some departmental prose justifies the remark of Mr. G. M. Young to Sir Ernest Gowers—" it just shows what Whitehall can do "—dwellers in other glasshouses, including the authors of learned books, will be the first to admit that they can do as badly—and worse.

SMALL CHANGE

In the light of what has been happening to the prices of such things as linoleum and smoked salmon, it would be churlish to complain at having to put one more penny into the slot when we telephone from a public kiosk. It is not only the loss of the penny that will trouble us, but also the difficulty of finding it in the first place. In the normal run of things pennies are plentiful, but a man has only to step inside a call-box to find that he has nothing but halfpennies and sixpenny pieces in his pocket. That trouble will now be aggravated, but we may console ourselves with the reminder that an earlier generation also had to find those three elusive pence, for the charge was not reduced to twopence until 1923.

For all the financial complications to which it may give rise the kiosk remains a friendly refuge. In the thirty-odd years of its existence it has appeared in a variety of guises. It can trace its descent from the wooden boxes which were set up at railway stations and other sheltered spots as early as 1912, but it was not until 1921 that a serious attempt at an outside kiosk was made. This was a cruder version of what we have to-day, with a wooden door and an ornamental roof surmounted by a spike. The model must be almost extinct—one is said still to be in existence at Chiswick—for, after experiments with thatched roofs and stamp-machines set in the back wall, it was superseded by the designs of SIR GILES GILBERT SCOTT, R.A., whose "Jubilee" kiosk of 1936, with its graceful lines, is the one in general use to-day. To the most critical it is inoffensive and to the wayfarer in distress it is a gladdening sight. The interior has, moreover, with its windows, its mirror and its shiny surfaces, the great advantage over earlier kiosks of being almost proof against the doodlers and scribblers.

The kiosk also makes a subtler appeal, for it figures prominently in the little dramas of our life. It brings comfort to the stranger in a city and to the isolated cottage. In war-time thousands of ex-civilians, banished to outlandish parts of the country, appreciated its value. For them it provided a link with home, and if the lighting was at times inadequate and the ventilation disappointing, they were not disposed to criticize. In peace it is to the kiosk we go with our stories of altered plans, broken ankles, and broken axles; it is from it that go forth the clandestine messages which must not be overheard. So long as this continues it may well be that we shall consider the service relatively cheap, even at the new price.

MERE STORYTELLERS

There is no such animal, said Mr. Somerset Maugham recently, as the mere storyteller. He also told the members of the National Book League, to whom he was speaking on "The Writer's Point of View," that all literature is escapist and "that is its charm." These two arguments, woven together with the skill of Mr. Somerset Maugham, make a provocative pattern. He challenges the aesthetic theory, fashionable at the moment, that writers of fiction must leave a message and busy themselves with sociology and economics and world affairs. They should, in his view, stick to their last, shaping and sewing together the most interesting tales that are in them. Their function is to give intelligent pleasure, and they will remain unskilful, however naturally talented they may be, unless they acquire the technique of the art of writing. A person who wants to be a painter goes to an art school, and an aspiring pianist takes lessons; but, in Mr. Somerset Maugham's experience of reading many manuscripts, it seldom occurs to those who want to be writers that they have anything to learn.

Those many people who have been beguiled in the library and in the theatre by the author of *Cakes and Ale* and *The Circle* may take him as the exception who proves his own rule. He might seem, so easily does he read and act, to have been a storyteller from the day of his birth in that home of well-constructed stories, Paris. Those who know his autobiography—and he has never written anything better—will remember with what pains he learnt his craft and how critically he has studied its old and modern masters. No writer of the last two generations has been more serious in the service of novel, short story, and play. His plea for escapism may, then, be treated as a carrying of the war into the enemy's country. The degree of truth in it can be judged by testing it against comments made by two of Mr. MAUGHAM's contemporaries. ARNOLD BENNETT maintained that, if we are not tired after reading, common sense is not in us. CHESTERTON distinguished between the eager man who wants to read a book and the tired man who wants a book to read. Escapism, seen through these glasses, turns out, after all, to be a strenuous exercise. The reader who is to enjoy the delights of being carried away by a work of fiction must learn to ride a spirited horse. If he wants to get full value out of his journey across imaginative country he must not ask for a back seat in a limousine.

How far demand for a " message "—for an earnest point of view—is justified needs to be carefully assessed. KIPLING, MR. MAUGHAM suggests, may sometimes be dismissed nowadays as a mere storyteller, but it is nearer the truth to say that his genius for storytelling is often forgotten by dull people, simply because they disapprove of his politics and his philosophy. MR. MAUGHAM recognizes this when he agrees that a novelist cannot help taking sides. The wide range and choice of sides were pleasantly brought out by MR. MAUGHAM in an exchange of letters he had with an American lady who asked him what her son at Harvard should do to fit himself for a career as a novelist. The answer she got was, " Give your son a thousand dollars a year for five years and tell him to go to the devil." When this advice, distasteful to a mother, had been explained to mean that all-round knowledge of the world would be useful the lady replied, " Miss Austen wrote her admirable novels without leaving the respectable circle in which she was born, and Mr. Henry James never to my knowledge moved in any world but that to which he was entitled by his birth and position." The thrust was shrewd and there is no defence against it except to conclude, as Mr. Maugham does, that all experience is grist to the writer's mill. If he is a storyteller, he will hold his readers enthralled by whatever theme has struck sparks out of him—whether or no he has a message.

Mr. MACMILLAN AND THE FAIRIES

If Mr. Harold Macmillan finds a fairy hopping on his knee when he first sits down in his new office at the Ministry of Housing he will know, better than any other Minister, how to deal with her. His long association, as a publisher, with Kipling will have taught him that fairies are not to be laughed at. No rewards must be expected from them if a housing estate goes up on Pook's Hill. This foreknowledge will be useful if what has happened in Ireland has reactions—as well it may—over here. An official announcement is just reported to have been made by an Irish local authority that " in order to give our people houses we will have to give in to the fairies." This surrender followed an assault by bulldozers on a site that belonged to the leprechauns. Workmen found the ground landlords busy on their traditional craft of shoemaking, which was abandoned to resist the trespass. Prudently, another site is being chosen. Up-to-date information about fairies is hard to come by, but two things about them are certain and they should both be borne in mind by Mr. Macmillan. The first is that fairies are quick movers. They can put a girdle round the earth in forty minutes, and, so, the news of their victory in Ireland must already be known in every fairy ring as far east as Romney Marsh. The second point is that fairies are highly emotional. Quick to resent injury, they are no less ready to press home an advantage and they have had every reason in late years to resent their neglect at British hands.

Oberon and Titania live largely as characters in a play and, for the rest, they are only heard about, behaving like hooligans, under the ugly Teutonic name of poltergeists. Too long have they been dismissed as whimsies.

In future they may assert their rights as town and country planners. If they are received sympathetically, this can be made to redound to the credit of the Government. Fairies have a record as builders that deserves to be recalled. Living rough themselves—content to lie in cowslip bells and never taking hurt in the wildest weather—they have some remarkable building feats to look back on.

They have run up a castle in a single night and they have, as quickly, put a roof on a byre large enough to hold as many cows as there are days in the year. Several English churches are known to have been the work of fairy builders. As employees they are not ideal. The long hours they are ready to put in, when the spirit moves them, is not the only thing that may bring them into conflict with trade union practice. They have been known to interfere with an architect, of whose style they disapproved, by removing, in one shift, his half-finished masterpiece. MR. MACMILLAN will have to handle this potential labour force tactfully, but, with Irish precedent in mind, he must avoid offending it. Trouble will be met if man-made council houses are defiantly erected in a wrong place and, then, plastered with warnings of "No Circulars, No Hawkers, No Fairies."

ON TALKING SHOP

There still persists a belief, not less widespread than quaint, that the British, in polite society at any rate, never talk shop. This is one of those fallacies which, when they first became current, must have taken root so quickly and so deeply in the world's folklore that nobody since then has quite liked to point out that they are wholly at variance with the ascertainable facts. These are, to put the thing in a nutshell, that the British rarely talk anything but shop. It is true that in more spacious, leisured, and commodious times this tendency was probably less marked than it is to-day, for to our forefathers life resembled rather an art in which every one was a dilettante than the arduous, intricate craft in which we now find ourselves absorbingly, though not very rewardingly, engaged. The price of fish or the scarcity of coke were not topics which, if broached in an Edwardian salon, would have given rise to a long and animated discussion; RUSKIN, dining out, would have listened but abstractedly to an exposition of the problems involved in obtaining a maidservant from Ireland; and one does not visualize HENRY JAMES being particularly interested by a comparison, among his fellow-guests, of their respective chances of getting a new car in less than five years. Yet it is subjects such as these which to-day monopolize much of our conversation, and they are really a rather degraded kind of shop, for life has somehow been transformed from an adventure into an administrative obstacle race, or perhaps into a crossword puzzle of which, since it is compulsory for all, every one is equally interested in the same clues. Living has become a business, and when we discuss its complex but stereotyped technique we are really very little better than business men talking shop.

Apart from this all the old forms of shop, and some new ones as well, flourish, and are in some cases encouraged to flourish. The hostess who invites a newly fledged Cabinet Minister to dinner does not do so in the hope that he will talk about the poetic drama, or the folk-music of Latin America; she hopes that he will talk shop, and she and all her guests will be very much disappointed if he does not. When we meet an explorer or a detective-inspector or a hypnotist we do not seek to elicit his views on the political situation or his opinions of the ballet; we want him to talk about his avocation.

There is, of course, a good deal to be said for the theory that it really takes two to talk shop. It is when two members of the same profession get going in the presence of others that the rest of the company begin to suffer. Their sufferings vary in intensity according to the nature of the profession concerned. While no hard and fast official grading of the different kinds of shop has ever been laid down, it may be said with a fair amount of certainty that legal shop is, owing to the fluency with which lawyers are trained to talk, peculiarly oppressive; that medical shop differs from military shop in that, while both are incomprehensible, one rather regrets not being able to understand the former; that theatrical shop always holds out the promise of being entertaining, but somehow rarely fulfils it; that farming shop almost comes into the category of an act of God; and that there is no such thing as political shop, only malicious gossip. But the subject is too vast to deal with, save very tentatively, here; and it remains only, as we take leave of it, to record respectful admiration of the ladies who, though by virtue of their station in life they suffer atrociously from having to listen to shop being talked, are often able to wreak on their tormentors a most frightful revenge by conversing, in their presence and at length, about clothes.

AND FRIEND

No thoughtful reader of the illustrated periodicals devoted to the activities of what used to be called Society can fail to have noted, and been grieved by, the virtual disappearance from their pages of a once familiar character. " Character," as a matter of fact, is the wrong word for what was really a minor role in which a succession of anonymous actors had their first, and in some cases it is to be feared their only, chance of making an impression on the public. They were the individuals —almost always male—who, having been photographed in the company of more celebrated persons—generally female—were described in the accompanying caption as " . . . and Friend." To the editors of the glossy publications in which he formerly appeared And Friend doubtless seemed uninteresting as well as insignificant ; the editors would have liked to have suppressed him altogether, as at the end of a drive, when the bag is laid out in a row, the head keeper stuffs into his pocket the humble, anomalous moorhen which came over with the pheasants and got shot by mistake. But the camera cannot lie, and there was And Friend leaning over the paddock rails beside the *débutante* of the season, escorting the glamorous Miss Mink through the crowded foyer at a first night, dancing (generally in pierrot's costume) with Lady Watter-Smasher at the fancy dress ball, or sun-bathing at Enfer Roc with Baroness " Tiny " Rumpelstiltskin. There he was, looking ever so slightly bemused and clutching a race-card, a souvenir programme, a champagne-glass, a shooting-stick, a yachting cap, or a noblewoman ; and there he had to stay. Now he has gone. Whither ? And why ?

The two questions can be answered—tentatively, of course—together. And Friend has lost his anonymity (and with it his powerful hold upon our curiosity and interest) because the staffs of the illustrated papers, in which he now drearily appears as Mr. G. Wednesday or as Captain R. P. Footle, are better at finding out the names of the people whose photographs they publish, and because their editors are more insistent that they should do so. But there may be a little more in it than that. And Friend is, theoretically at any rate, a beneficiary from the process of levelling up. His former appellation implied that he was a nobody, and you cannot have nobodies nowadays. It is not done. So And Friend has been promoted, kicked upstairs into nonymity (if there is such a word), identified, provided with an initial or two (generally his own), and expunged for ever from the short list of people whose photographs in the illustrated papers we look at more than once.

As And Friend he was an interesting, even a romantic, character. He looked no dimmer than the other men whose likenesses appeared on adjacent pages. He was always appropriately dressed. Why (one simply could not help wondering) this incognito? Was he afraid of being compromised? Or was he perhaps in the Secret Service? Was Miss Mink ashamed of being seen with him or he ashamed of being seen with Miss Mink? Had he refused to divulge his identity or had the editor decided to suppress it? Who, in any case, was he? Fascinated, we scrutinized his slightly owlish features and speculated about his social background. We do so no longer. The yashmak of anonymity has been lifted, and the faces of Mr. Wednesday and Captain Footle hold none of the mysterious challenge which distinguished And Friend's. When he was a nobody he was somebody. Now, as far as we are concerned, he is merely a waste of newsprint.

LENIN'S TEA-STRAINER

It was in February, 1916, that LENIN and his wife settled in Zürich to continue gestating the Russian Revolution. Their funds were low and they began by living in a humble boarding-house. " Ilyitch," Krupskaya wrote, " liked the simplicity of the service, the fact that the coffee was served in a cup with a broken handle, that we ate in the kitchen, that the conversation was simple." Though the place had a raffish charm, the pair soon realized that it was unsatisfactory. Their fellow-guests were a queer set. One, though he did not talk much, showed, " by the casual phrases he uttered that he was of an almost criminal type." Such an atmosphere was, they decided, unsettling for revolutionaries and they moved out and took lodgings with a shoemaker's family in a rambling sixteenth-century house in the Spiegelgasse. Not until long after his bearded down-at-heel visitor with the sharp inquiring eyes and the mania for writing letters had come and gone did the shoemaker discover that he had been living with history.

Highly placed foreigners in smart cars drove up to the old man's front door and asked if they could inspect his spare room. They offered him untold wealth—in roubles or Swiss francs—for the bedstead, the washbasin, the sticks of furniture. He was obstinate and refused to sell; it was his wife's furniture and he had not found his taciturn lodger impressive. For years the shoemaker withheld these relics from the sixth of the world that was aching to venerate them. He was a simple man and would appear to have been unable, to the end of his life, to understand what all the fuss was about. Earlier this year he died. Now it has been reported that a number of the personal belongings that LENIN had used in Zürich—

his tea-strainer, a glass from which he drank tea, and two knives—have been sent to the East German Republic as the result of a "cultural exchange" with the Swiss Government. In return the Swiss have received twenty-three pieces of Chinese sculpture and pottery lent to East German museums.

Where such different values are in question it is hard to say which side has got the best of the bargain. Perhaps, in the present clash of world ideologies, the neutral and pacific Swiss may be better placed to appreciate the aesthetic mysteries of T'ang and Ming. Certainly the tea-strainer has been placed where its totemistic power will be most intensely felt. What would LENIN himself, it may be asked, have thought of the exchange? His aesthetic sense was not highly developed and his only form of cultural amusement was reading. On the question of exchanging his valueless impedimenta for the emblems of *rentier* culture there can be little doubt of his reaction. He would have sold the pottery at once. It would have been used to finance *Iskra* or to endow a new printing press. To that hard and analytical Marxist intelligence there would have been an insane element of surplus value about the whole transaction. His comments on the East Berliners' foolishness would surely have been scathing and in his best manner. "Once again," one can hear him exclaiming, "the workers have made themselves the dupes of the *petite bourgeoisie*!"

THE GHOSTS ARE GOING

Night falls early, the wind whines ; leaves, heard but not seen, scurry before us as we come towards the lighted windows of our homes. Darkness, with which we had little to do all summer, is reinstated as a factor in our lives. Another winter has moved in on us. We think of winter as a rather old-fashioned season, full of old-fashioned things like firelight and eiderdowns and draughts, pink coats and card-tables and the ring of axes in the frosty air. In the country especially, winter does not seem to have changed very much, and the rather inadequate resources which we mobilize against its *longueurs* and its inconveniences include few novelties of importance.

In the ranks of winter, however, there has been one casualty of note. What has happened to the ghosts ? We still tell, we still occasionally read, stories about them ; but there was a time when the darkness and the sound of the wind in the eaves automatically turned our minds to ghosts, and that time would seem to have passed. Few of us, in those days, really expected to see a ghost ; but as the advance guards of winter closed in on us we could not help sparing a thought, even if it was only an academic or a facetious one, for the apparitions who were supposed to be in operational reserve. That does not happen now, and it is scarcely to be wondered at. Ghosts—who, of course, have no vote—have been overlooked by the Welfare State just at the time when their interests, threatened on every side, most needed safeguarding.

No class in the community has had to face a more acute or delicate housing problem. The technical difficulties of haunting a prefab must be wellnigh insuperable, and, though the type of accommodation to which ghosts are accustomed is still available here and there, much of it is occupied by the Civil Service, whose hours of duty seldom overlap with those of even the most conscientious spook. There can be precious little satisfaction in clanking your chains all over the west wing when there is nothing there except a lot of tea-cups and a number of graphs, all showing a downward trend; and in those mansions or castles which are still in the hands of their original owners the more sensitive type of phantom is deterred from doing his stuff by the fear that the film rights in it will be sold over his head, whether he has one or not. Flood-lighting has kept many battlements clear of spectres, while others, materializing as usual in the library, have been piqued and frustrated by their inability to distract the attention of the occupants from their television set. Altogether these have been hard times for the small, but exclusive, supernatural community in our midst; and, though we may congratulate ourselves that with the change of Government there will soon be a new spirit abroad in the country, we must recognize the hard fact that, unless something is done to protect the interests of the ghosts, a lot of the old spirits in the country will soon be abroad.

A FLOCK OF PELICANS

Londoners were saddened to learn not long since of the deaths of Peter and Paul, those two amiable and portly pelicans who have moved with slow and shambling gait, or simply stood—between them for sixty-three years—on the lawns of St. James's Park. Indeed there have been pelicans in St. James's standing, waddling, and occasionally emitting a raucous guffaw, since the days when CHARLES II went strolling by three centuries ago. Peter himself, who must have been nearly sixty, came from Karachi to Kew in 1898 and moved to St. James's in 1903. He resembled a quiet old gentleman, who, having long since ceased to worry about his girth, has just slipped in a pound or two of Dover sole, and is content merely to wait and feel it doing him good. Paul—a younger fellow, who came from North America between the wars—is said to have consumed also his full five pounds of fish a day. Perhaps that was why he gazed a trifle glaucously at passers by.

Their passing, however, is to have not one, it seems, but several happy endings. No sooner had the news crossed the Atlantic than the warm-hearted people of Texas resolved to offer in place of Peter and Paul, Gal, Ves, Ton, and Tex, who were duly whisked into an aeroplane and escorted forthwith to London by MR. JAMES CARTER, News Editor of the *Galveston News*, as "Ambassador to the Park of St. James in charge of Pelican Affairs," with instructions from the GOVERNOR of Texas to deliver them to MR. CHURCHILL. Gal, Ves, Ton, and Tex are apparently the smaller brown American pelican (*Pelecanus occidentalis*), though they might turn white later, which for Londoners, after Peter and Paul, must remain the traditional colour for a pelican. The

State of Louisiana, which loves and cherishes the pelican as its official bird, was dismayed to hear of the precipitate action of Texas. No less warm-hearted, but acting, as no doubt befitted " the Pelican State," at a somewhat more measured tempo, Louisiana approached the British Government through normal diplomatic channels. In umbrage at the action taken by Texas, it has protested to the British Embassy in Washington, claiming that Louisiana should have the privilege of presenting pelicans to the park. It offered a pair of the larger white American pelicans (*Pelecanus erythrorhynchos*), which the Foreign Office have instructed the Consul-General in New Orleans gratefully to accept.

The unfortunate *malentendu* between the two American states is not, however, the only international repercussion. It appears that one of the first tasks of the Commonwealth Relations Office under MR. CHURCHILL'S Government was to request the United Kingdom High Commissioner in Pakistan to seek the cooperation of the Pakistani authorities to restore the line of pelicans which their Peter had so long upheld. While gestures of Anglo-American good will from Texas and Louisiana are appreciated in Pakistan, it is felt regrettable that Whitehall in a matter of such ancient tradition should look outside the Commonwealth. The AMIR of Pakistan's premier princely state has accordingly now offered pelicans from Bahawalpur—presumably, like Peter, large white pelicans with black stripes (*Pelecanus onocrotalus*). In the meantime, one further pelican has arrived from a private donor in Nairobi. This is the red or pink-backed pelican (*Pelecanus rufescens*), described as of medium size and a pretty pale cinnamon in colour. Truly Londoners may rejoice that the tradition of Peter and Paul and CHARLES II will live at least, it may be assumed, until the end of the century, and the donors may rest assured that Londoners and many others are touched and grateful at so much world-wide generosity.

NON-GESTICULANTS

The right of every individual to self-expression is very clearly recognized in modern society. We go out of our way to encourage it in children, and we accept the need for it as an excuse for all sorts of aberrations in grown-ups. If a young gentleman grows a beard or keeps an ocelot, if a young lady smokes cigars or takes up sculpture, we say, often with justice, that they are expressing themselves; and the efforts of artists and poets to do the same are automatically entitled to our respect, though we are occasionally rather bewildered by them. In these circumstances it seems odd that in this country one aid to self-expression, regarded elsewhere as practically indispensable, is nowadays almost wholly neglected. The use of gestures, to make plain or to emphasize one's meaning, seems to be obsolescent in Great Britain, though whether this is equally true of Northern Ireland is less certain.

At the very outset of our careers we were all much addicted to gestures and lay for long periods upon our backs, waving our arms and legs imperiously in the air. Perhaps we overdid it a bit in those early days. Now, at any rate, we seem to have abandoned almost entirely this useful aid to self-expression, and when we see foreigners relying on it we speak of them, with pitying contempt, as "gesticulating." Why we should detect something slightly ludicrous in our fellow-beings when they (in the dictionary's words) "make lively or energetic motions with the limbs or body," it is impossible to say. But we do; and our own range of gesture is remarkably narrow. We may permit ourselves from time to time a shrug of the shoulders; but it is a mere anatomical *frisson* compared with the convulsions to which

Continental torsos are subjected on such occasions. Our technique when either shaking or nodding our heads is languorous and effete compared with that employed in most other parts of the world; and the nearest most of us ever come to making a full-blooded gesture is when we wave our umbrella rather awkwardly at a taxi.

Were the British always so (as it were) mealy-limbed? According to the artists, no. Generals were constantly waving their swords in the air with graceful abandon. Men shook their fists, put their hands on their hearts; ladies covered their faces with their hands or stretched their arms upwards in despair or admiration. One has only got to go to a historical drama to see how ossified our behaviour has become since we gave up slapping our thighs, clapping each other on the shoulder, dusting ourselves with lace handkerchiefs, tapping our snuff-boxes, and bowing almost to the ground every time we met a lady. Like the penguins, who could not be bothered to fly and gradually lost the power of doing so, the British are becoming non-gesticulants. It would be interesting to know if the penguins adopt the same attitude to other birds as we do to foreigners and if, when they see the petrels and the albatrosses dipping or whirling overhead, they say to each other with superior smiles, "Wonderful, isn't it, how some people never seem to mind making themselves ridiculous!"

SNAIL'S PROGRESS

There is a point at which worms traditionally turn, but hitherto nothing has been heard of insult or injury up with which, in the Churchillian phrase, snails will not put. They have more than enough to complain about even in a country where they are not widely esteemed as a table delicacy, for the gardener joins forces against them with his natural enemies the birds. Now they are reported to be hitting back. An advance raiding party is said to have been surprised chewing a picture postcard in the village postbox at Merthyr Mawr. The personnel in this action numbered only three, but they evidently belonged to a strong hostile force. Observers report that dozens of snails are alerted and have inflicted considerable damage on their objective. Postcards are being made illegible, and counter-attack has only worsened the strategic situation. Rags soaked in paraffin and reinforced by a sprinkling of D.D.T. have carried on the bad work of the snails against love letters and income-tax forms without driving back the invaders. The reported cry is " Still they come," and an official is quoted as having remarked with stoic calm that " Snails in village postboxes are one of the routine problems we have to face." Civilian reaction to this news of battle will depend on the zeal of each individual for writing and receiving letters.

A minority of diehard conscientious objectors to correspondence may agree with THOREAU, who once confessed that he could easily do without the Post Office, for he never received more than one or two letters in his life that were worth the postage. THOREAU had more resources in himself than most people are endowed with, and his unsociable sentiment is not generally shared. Hope springs eternal as the postman appears and, even though he brings so many bills and circulars and so few cheques and invitations, the round on which he drops nothing through the door is a disappointment. New interest will be given to his visits if the snail campaign spreads and there is a sporting chance that the final demand from the Gas Board may arrive with its figures eaten away. On the other hand, more pleasant information may go too and the balance, for those to whom letters are addressed, will be unfavourable.

For letter writers, yet another excuse for putting off the dreary business of answering has been provided. Who can be expected to take the trouble to express himself aptly or to take the risk of enclosing a cheque, if all his efforts may end in a snail's maw? "Your inquiry would have been acknowledged long ago had the postboxes in this district not been in enemy occupation." The excuse has about it an engaging novelty. The only correspondents who will take no pleasure in it are the young and the engaged. For a few years, in youth and adolescence, sprawling pages are exchanged among friends and, again, under the sweet stimulus of being in love, the flow of words comes easily. At other stages, letter writing has ceased to be an art. The old theory that it is the most delightful way of wasting time has gone out of fashion. The snails in their drive to make correspondence more difficult can count on many quislings among men and women who, breaching the united human front, will wish them good browsing in the postboxes.

THE CARRIAGE WAITS

Small children who go out to a party have to be fetched back from it; so much, even in the worst-regulated households, is almost axiomatic. Some fathers occasionally volunteer, some—perhaps less rarely—are detailed for this duty. Few, until they have performed it several times, realize in how many delicate social problems it is liable to involve them. In order to fetch children from a party it is first of all necessary to know where the party is taking place; and many a father before now has discovered, on the very eve of setting out on his errand of mercy, that he has been inadequately briefed on this fundamental point. "Ursula's birthday party"—that, he knows, is the social function which his offspring are attending; and Ursula he identifies with reasonable certainty as the pretty little girl who had a sort of fit at the fireworks. But who are Ursula's parents, and where do they live? His mind is a blank on the subject. He seems to remember being told that Ursula has a pony—or was it a Siamese cat? But that is not enough to go on, on a dark winter's night; and if his spouse is absent he is often obliged to make several anxious telephone calls to other parents of the younger set in the neighbourhood.

Less than half an hour later, having parked his car in a flower-bed, he has gained admittance to the scene of revelry. The continuous din of tin whistles, mouth-organs, and hooters is punctuated by the intermittent bursting of balloons, each explosion being followed by a wail of grief and rage. "You've come," says Ursula's mother, advancing in a slightly *distrait* manner through all this pandemonium, "for yours?" This is the moment when, if every one's luck is in, the man's children make their appearance, thus enabling Ursula's mother to identify him and dispelling his own suspicions that he has come to the wrong house.

His children, after unloading on him a selection of paper hats and balloons and enjoining him to take the greatest care of them, are led away to be prepared for the homeward journey. The man finds himself becalmed in a group of ladies with whom his acquaintance, if any, is slight. He feels—needlessly, no doubt—at a disadvantage. The only possible topic of conversation is, obviously, children, and these ladies know so much more than he does about (so to speak) the points of a child, are so infinitely better informed about which children belong to whom, that he cannot hope to say anything intelligent or even sensible. He feels out of place, and this feeling is not lessened by the calculated and rather pitying look with which the ladies assess him. "I wonder," each seems to be asking herself (and no doubt they will all ask each other the moment he has gone), "why his wife didn't come? He looks so lost and unhappy. I wonder ——" But at last his children reappear, looking dissipated but cheerful. "Say goodbye." They do so, with infinite reluctance; and the man, as he shepherds them out to the car, feels that he has made unnecessarily heavy weather of a really perfectly simple operation.

THE RULES OF THE GAME

"Won't Brooke let me play?" Tom Brown asked eagerly of East on his first day at Rugby. "Not he," East answered with scorn. "Why, you don't know the rules; you'll be a month learning them." Readers of the article which appeared in *The Times* recently on the rise of Rugby football may think that Tom would have taken years to learn the rules as they have varied in the different schools to which has spread the Rugby gospel. And yet those early codes were crude and primitive in the extreme, and allowed loopholes for endless argument compared with the far more elaborate one of to-day. It has been the same with other games. In COLONEL RAIT KERR'S engaging little book on the laws of cricket there is a reproduction of the earliest laws of 1744 as printed on what Mr. Stiggins would have called a "moral pocket-handkerchief, blending select tales with woodcuts." The body of the handkerchief is occupied by a picture of a game in progress, and the laws are squeezed into sixteen small panels round the border. In the code of 1947 there are forty-seven rules and a similar phenomenon is to be seen in the rules of golf. In the St. Andrews code of 1754 there were thirteen rules; in that of 1949 there are forty-four, many of them with a number of sub-sections.

This progress to complexity is doubtless equally inevitable in other games. Persons of robust intellect assert that we should unscramble the omelet and return to the beautifully simple codes of our ancestors, but they have seldom tried their hand at law-making. If they had they might change their tune. Regrettable though it is in many ways, it is practically impossible to go back. Those who yearn for primitive things do not perhaps always realize how primitive they were and to what disputes they must constantly have led. When E. M. Grace was at school at Long Ashton he was, in the absence of any umpires, unanimously given out l.-b.-w. by the fielding side. He went out, but brought the game to a premature close by carrying the stumps away with him. In more modern times the story is told of Big Crawford, the famous Musselburgh caddie, when some question of law arose in a professional match. " Well," he announced, " it's the rule of the game, and here," pointing to his vast fist, " is the referee." Both are pleasant pictures, but surely bad precedents.

The rules of a game are made gradually as problems and emergencies arise not hitherto provided for. Those who were there will doubtless remember an occasion on St. Andrew's Day at Eton when that very, very rare event, a goal, appeared to have been scored at the wall. The ball hit the door in Good Calx with a triumphant thump, up went the referee's stick, back ran the players to the middle of the wall. Then it appeared that one of the defending side had alleged, no doubt truthfully, that the ball in its flight had unseen touched his finger-tips ; further that the referee and the umpires had decided that very morning at breakfast that in case of such a claim the goal should be disallowed. The wall game is an esoteric mystery of no very general interest, but here was a good example of how rules come into being. We have seen something of the same kind in the summer of 1951 when Hutton was given out for having in perfect innocence of intention obstructed the field. New sets of circumstances are for ever arising and the cry for perfect fairness in all of them grows ever more insistent. A little more roughness and readiness of legislation might be a good thing, but when we learn that Marlborough and Clifton did not meet again at football for some thirty years on account of a little argument about " hacking over " it seems that too high a price can be paid for the primitive.

AN AMERICAN OCCASION

A feast day on which it is worth while to make merry should have a significant basis. That is why Thanksgiving Day means so much to the citizens of the United States who celebrated it yesterday all over the world, not least in this country. The amenities of the occasion, the roast turkey and cranberry sauce and the pumpkin pie, would lose their special flavour if they had not been preceded, earlier in the day, by the reading of the PRESIDENT'S Proclamation with the memories it evokes of ancient hazards faced and overcome. Pride in the Pilgrim Fathers is combined, for exiles and for Americans at home, with humility at the thought of a providential escape from famine. The pioneers, having crossed the ocean in their little ships, found that " notwithstand all their great paines and industrie and ye great hops of a large cropp, the Lord seemed to blast and take away the same." No wonder that, when the harvest was, after all, garnered, they were thankful and that their descendants have not forgotten this deliverance.

Nowadays the tradition that on Thanksgiving Day the grey haired New Englander sees round his board the old broken links of affection restored is honoured from coast to coast. Schools and universities give holidays and families reunite. There were growing pains before this custom was established. The South adopted it only midway through last century and, for some time, the actual day remained doubtful. LINCOLN began the practice of a National Proclamation, fixing the fourth Thursday in November, but he had no power to order a holiday in the various states, and, just before the last war, PRESIDENT ROOSEVELT made a controversial attempt to halt the movable feast at November 23.

Many Governors refused to accept this date, preferring November 30, and a few authorized the celebration of both dates. In 1951 PRESIDENT TRUMAN was able to refer to the joint resolution of Congress, approved in 1941, designating the fourth Thursday in November in each year as Thanksgiving Day.

An advantage of being a comparatively young country is that national beginnings do not lose themselves in the mists of history. What the United States has settled could not be matched in Britain. It might be pleasant to eat oysters and to drink Falernian—if Italy could still send some over from her cellars—in rejoicing over the failure of the stormy Channel seas to drown the Roman legions. A gargantuan meat ration, washed down with mead, would go well in honour of the first landfall made by Saxons. Tripe, cooked in the mode of Caen, could, with other French delicacies, appear annually at table on the day of WILLIAM'S conquest at Hastings. Those festivities, unfortunately, would divide the island. Few people would know which camp they were in, Roman or British, Saxon or Norman. The background of a feast that went with a swing would be lacking. The Americans have in Thanksgiving Day a reason that cannot be imitated for enjoying themselves and, at the same time, for looking back into their past.

WITH A LOW, MOCKING LAUGH

It is exceptionally difficult to evaluate the achievement of the Italian who, according to a news agency report, has invented a spy-proof envelope. One's first, unthinking reaction is one of casual gratitude. " Bound to come in useful," mutters the ordinary citizen. It is only on reflection that an element of doubt creeps in. What is a spy-proof envelope? If he had invented a fly-proof envelope we should understand him to have designed an envelope into which it was impossible for flies to gain admission; but even the smallest spy cannot get inside even the largest envelope and it is difficult to see what advantage would accrue to him if he could.

A burglar-proof safe is a safe which a burglar cannot, in theory anyhow, open; and an envelope with similar properties would undoubtedly create alarm and despondency, and perhaps even some marginal unemployment, among secret agents. But if a spy cannot open an envelope, neither, surely, will the addressee be able to, and it seems pointless to send secret documents all over the place if the recipients are never going to be able to read them. A moth-proof envelope—well, here for a moment one seems to see a ray of light, for that would be an envelope which moths could not eat, and many a spy in a tight corner has swallowed the plans of the fortress. But this will not do either, for no spy worthy of his spirit-gum eats the envelope as well; to do so would not only be unnecessary and injurious to the health, but would be regarded in espionage circles as ostentatious and ill-bred.

Across some, though not the most perspicuous, minds may flash the idea that the envelope's spy-proof qualities perhaps reside in the fact that you cannot write on it in invisible ink; or rather that, if you do, nobody (or alternatively everybody) will be able to read what you have written. Invisible ink, however, though an indispensable accessory to a career in clandestine intelligence, has its limitations; and one of the things it is absolutely no good for at all is addressing envelopes. But stay! If the seeker after truth (or even after probability) returns to the original report he will note that the invention is described, not merely as a spy-proof envelope, but as "a spy-proof envelope which will foil even the cleverest Mata Hari." Now at last we are getting somewhere. Everybody knows what female spies do with secret documents; they thrust them into their corsages, generally accompanying the action with a low, mocking laugh. One does not have to belong to M.I.5 to realize what a severe blow will have been struck against this old-established practice if the new envelopes are made of sandpaper, or even of Harris tweed. Female spies are brave, enduring people. Like the Spartan boy with a fox gnawing his midriff, they may well be able to face the world boldly with the equivalent of a loofah wedged in their *décolletage*; but we shall probably hear less of those low, mocking laughs.

FAULTLESSLY DRESSED

Among the many reasons for believing that a man is a bigger fool than his wife is that he knows so few of the right words for what he wears. Creators, dreaming in Paris or Mayfair of new fashions, can be sure that, when they join the ladies, they may safely ride their technical vocabulary on a snaffle. If they have a word for it—from the top of the hat to the heel of the shoe—the ladies will understand. The lexicon of the wardrobe on its distaff side is ABC to a school girl, as it is Greek to her father. He shows up no better in the language of his own clothes. He is unaware that authority has laid down that the bottom button of his waistcoat should be unbuttoned only if there are at least five buttons above it. He does not even know how many buttons he has on his waistcoat. The spokesmen of Savile Row woo him, if they are wise, in much the same way as missionaries had to deal with a savage audience that was only one step ahead of the monkeys in noises that made sense. Men are being taught at the moment that this is the season of the backward glancing Mid-Century look. Their jackets are to be lengthened, their trousers narrowed and their cuffs turned back. Not to look Edwardian is not to look up to date. So far the receptive listener is in the picture. He may not want his trousers narrower or tighter than they already are, but he understands what is expected of him. Then he is told that the "drape," a product of his age, has been retained for comfort.

At this point the attentive savages and their sartorial confessor begin to get at cross purposes. Nobody likes to admit that he has not the slightest idea that his suit has a drape. There is silence, broken by the news that the centre vent may, without shame, be kept. It is hardly likely to be that familiar hole in the middle of the pocket through which sixpences and latch keys take a header into the wide open spaces of the lining, but what else is it? What are the differences between bluff patch, welted outside and jetted and flapped pockets? How do gauntlet-cuffed jackets distinguish themselves from those threatened with turned back cuffs? If a member of the tribe who had stolen a march on his fellows strolled into the circle with his thumbs in a step-collared waistcoat, what would he look like, and what if, above it, he were wearing a semi-fitted overcoat with a fly front?

These are mysteries and they darken if the new world is brought in to redress the balance of the old. Meagre though male vocabulary is about clothes, Englishmen and Americans do not share it. An Englishman walking down Bond Street in vest and pants would be a figure out of a nightmare. An American doing the same along Broadway would merely be in his shirtsleeves. Suspenders worn in Britain round the legs are promoted across the Atlantic to maintaining the security of trousers. How difficult it all seems was shown the other day by an American who has for long kept a deliciously perceptive eye on the British scene. MR. CHRISTOPHER MORLEY reproaches us for still calling that " distressing garment " in which we swim a bathing dress. An Englishman charged with this offence is puzzled. He knows that he does not say bathing dress, but the term is familiar to him, and, when he comes to think of it, he is not sure what he does say. Bathing costume sounds wrong, and swim suit and trunks sound worse. When the " distressing garment " has, as so often happens, been lost by its owner, in what words does he reproach his family for having hidden it? Let him close his eyes and speak aloud, and he will find himself saying plaintively, " Has anyone seen my bathing things? " There is nothing to be done with so hopeless an addict of Basic English.

AGAIN THE ABOMINABLE SNOWMAN

Man has a natural longing for the strange in general and for monsters in particular, and it is one of the saddest conditions of a civilization that is continually eating up more and more of the world's surface that only in the most remote places—the loftiest of mountains and the deepest of waters—does that longing still retain any hope of satisfaction. It is with rising hope that the reader receives, from the snows of Everest, the latest news of that king of monsters, the Abominable Snowman. One advantage which the Snowman has over all rivals is that he leaves his footprints behind him—as MR. ERIC SHIPTON'S remarkable photographs, published in *The Times*, demonstrate. It is in fact by his footprints alone, found in many parts of the Himalayan mountains, that the Snowman is known to European observers. It was LIEUTENANT-COLONEL C. K. HOWARD-BURY, in his account of the 1921 reconnaissance of Mount Everest, who first introduced this elusive creature to western readers. He then told how at a height of over 20,000 feet he found, among tracks of hares and foxes, " one that looked like a human foot." He thought it was probably caused by a wolf, but the coolies at once proclaimed it to be that of " ' The Wild Man of the Snows ' to which they gave the name of Metohkangmi, ' the Abominable Snow Man ' "—who from then on was secure of his place in literature if not in science.

Since then many accounts have recorded the tracks seen by European climbers and the stories told of the Snowman by various native peoples, who in the past never claimed to have seen him, since to see him was, by all accounts, to die. In some legends he is a terrible ape-like creature, eating yaks and men, and walking—as a minor macabre touch—with toes pointing inwards. In other legends the Snowmen were lonely spirits of women who had died in childbirth or of people who had suffered violent deaths, and they were not evil unless provoked. The scientists, trying to identify the footsteps, have differed almost as much in their diagnosis. They have suggested langur monkeys, wolves, even otters—and, perhaps with the greatest probability, a race of brown bear, *Ursus arctos isabellinus*. Opinion in favour of the brown bear hardened greatly as a result of an article by MR. F. S. SMYTHE in November, 1937, and adherents of more romantic theories have been able to do little more since then than fight a somewhat dispirited rearguard action. They may, perhaps, gain some heart from the testimony of one of MR. SHIPTON'S Sherpa porters that he had seen a " yeti " (another name for the Snowman) at twenty-five yards distance (without dying) and that it was covered with reddish-brown hair save for its face. Most people, however, will—even if a little sadly—think that the main point of interest is whether MR. SHIPTON'S latest article and photographs do or do not give further support to the bear theory—which has in its favour some curious legends that regard the bear almost as a kind of man, or at least as a king above all other beasts. No doubt one day a trained observer will actually see a Snowman—whatever he may be—taking one of his long lonely walks across the snow, and that will settle it. The world will have one mystery less.

REFLECTIONS IN A SHAVING MIRROR

A man who spends five minutes every morning in shaving is a prisoner to brush and razor for more than two months of an average lifetime. For sixty-six days, working a twenty-four hour day, he does, between the ages of seventeen and seventy, penance before the mirror. He is, if a random poll taken among males in the shaving age bracket be accepted, rather a quick worker. There are restless, unphilosophic types, impatient of routine and scornful of soap, who claim to dry shave themselves in three minutes. Their life sentence is only forty days and, in a year, they are let off with a mere eighteen hours on the job. Others, more meditative or with chins more stubbornly blue, ruefully admit that it takes them twenty minutes before they are ready to appear at the breakfast table looking—at least from the chin upwards—like guardsmen on parade. They let themselves in for the appalling vigil at the wash basin of nine months (in round figures and ignoring, with LORD RANDOLPH CHURCHILL, the damned dots).

These reflections are prompted by the exhibition at the Science Museum, of razors, ancient and modern, from stone through bronze and steel to electricity. The thought of primitive man, sprucing himself for a meet of the woolly rhinoceros hunt on a cold December morning with the edge of his flint razor a bit jagged, makes the atomic age feel like a bed of roses. It may be dismissed in favour of wondering how far even the Astronomer Royal would get among the statistics of days and hours devoted by mankind through history to this perpetual warfare against hair on the face. Old campaigners though we are, we have still to agree on the best tools and the best way of keeping the mind awake while they are being used. Electricity might have been expected to produce a magic wand of a razor, and some people assert fiercely that it has, but others continue to swear by a cut-throat. The middle party, staunching the little wounds inflicted by the so-called " safety " and debating the hundred and one unsatisfactory ways of disposing of the blades, envies both these extremes. A cut-throat would be ideal if it did not, in clumsy hands, become a lethal weapon when sharp and a feeble one when an attempt has been made to hone it. An electric razor would be no less enviable in the same hands if only it could be persuaded not to glide over the stubble, tickling like the feet of a butterfly and not hurting a single hair.

Shavers by all three methods unite in wishing that they belonged to the minority which finds stimulus in going through the familiar, automatic movements. Somebody learned a language a year by propping up a grammar beside the mirror. Somebody else found inspiration at the same dreary moment of the daily round for the jokes that later set music-halls in a roar. Another, not without reputation since, learned by heart his early political speeches. There are those who tell us that they are able to plan the order of the business that lies immediately before them, to remember letters they ought to have written and to work out in their heads how much will be left over to spend on Christmas after inescapable January bills have been taken into consideration. No brand of efficiency is more irritating to the unself-disciplined than that of the man who makes the most of shaving time. There is no escape in relaxation. Singing, suitable for the bath, leads to punishment and to spots of blood, descending treacherously and by delayed action on to the collar, if it be indulged in while the razor is being plied. Facing the years of repetitive labour ahead, there is no refuge for the ungifted shaver, not even—if he looks realistically at his mirrored chin—in a nice bushy beard.

ECHOES OF CHRISTMAS PAST

There is nothing like time for bringing together oddly assorted things, and in the little exhibition now open in the Museum of the Public Record Office time has been given a double innings. First, the official records of seven centuries and more have been attracted, through various channels, to the great building in Chancery Lane; and, secondly, a clever picking has been made, for the occasion, of such of them as refer to Christmas. The result is a highly curious miscellany which ranges, within no more than thirteen documents or groups of documents, from KING JOHN to the reign of QUEEN VICTORIA, from religion to the circumnavigation of the globe, and from playbills to pies. All turn, somehow, upon the festival of Christmas. There is even among them one anti-Christmas pronouncement—a Commonwealth document of December 26, 1650, in which the Council of State complains " that there was a very wilfull and strict observation of the day commonly called Christmasse day " in London and Westminster " by a general keeping of their shops shut up," and calls upon Parliament for " further provisions for the abolishing and punishing of those old superstitious observations."

It is something of a mental effort to realize that so Scroogeian an attitude was once, though not (as the document itself shows) general, at least held by an influential body of very worthy men. More cheerful, or more gracious, views prevailed, however, at most periods. Feasting, as might be supposed, figures largely in the picture and, as always, the amount which our ancestors were prepared to eat seems astonishing to the modern Englishman. Even in its own time KING JOHN's order at Christmas, 1206, for 1,500 chickens, 5,000 eggs, twenty oxen, a hundred pigs, and a hundred sheep, to be delivered at Winchester, softened though it was in the comforting rhythms of the Latin language, must have caused some alarm in the *entourage* of the SHERIFF of SOUTHAMPTON, who was apparently the local food officer of the time. The citizen of to-day, who intends to be tolerably merry this year on a rationed dietary can only sigh, on reading an early seventeenth-century recipe " For six Minst pyes of an Indifferent biggnesse " which includes " a Loyne of fatt Mutton, with a little of a Legg of Veale to mynce with it," for the passing of more opulent days.

Yet feasting is not by any means all that these Christmas documents reveal. They show us the accounts for the plays and masques acted, by five companies, before QUEEN ELIZABETH at this season in 1573. They show us, too, CAPTAIN JAMES COOK, on his last voyage, in 1777, celebrating the day far across the world, and naming the spot Christmas Island in honour of the occasion. Nor is the religious significance of the festival forgotten, and certainly the most delightful of the documents shown is the manuscript of a fifteenth-century carol beginning

> *Puer nobis natus est de virgine Maria*
> Lordyngs be glad bothe more and lesse
> I bryng you tydyngs of grette gladnesse
> As Gabriel ber [bear] us wittnes
> *Causa dico quia*
> *Puer nobis natus est de virgine Maria.*

And so, with those charming macaronics echoing in his mind, the visitor may leave the exhibition and, strolling southwards into Fleet Street, wonder whether this Christmas is likely to bring him anything else as sincere and touching as that echo from five centuries ago.

THE PET-SITTER

The young lady who, through an advertisement in a New York newspaper, is offering her services as a " pet-sitter " may be supposed to have done what every Christmas shopper is trying, rather hopelessly, to do ; she has fulfilled a long-felt want. The tyranny exercised by pets over their owners is peculiarly harsh and complete. Other tyrants can be deposed or overthrown ; but you cannot overthrow a Pekingese or depose a canary. Nor are the victims of oppression sustained and comforted by the knowledge, which helps to alleviate their sufferings at the hands of small children, that one day their oppressors will go away to boarding-school. Some dogs, it is true, are sent away in their youth to be trained, but not for long. The average pet, once it has established a bridgehead, is there for keeps.

The young lady, clearly a sanguine type, professes herself ready to invigilate over " any type of pet." New York does not strike one as a city very well adapted to the requirements of pet-lovers ; the duty of letting out the cat, irksome enough in a suburban villa, must be very onerous to people living in the top-hamper of a sky-scraper. But the citizens are an enterprising and imaginative lot, unlikely to be deterred by administrative difficulties from seeking solace in the companionship of dumb or anyhow inarticulate friends. The young lady is in little danger of lacking engagements. She may, on the other hand, encounter a diversity of perils if she accepts them.

Everybody knows what a baby-sitter is supposed to do (though, curiously enough, hardly anybody except the baby ever sees her do it). She simply sits with or near (but never on) the baby, which with any luck is asleep. She ministers, when necessity arises, to its needs, prevents it from being smothered by the cat, and in the event of the house catching fire—a contingency preoccupation with which sometimes makes young mothers rather unreliable partners at the bridge table—it is expected of the baby-sitter that she will remove the baby to a place of safety. The duties of a pet-sitter are clearly analogous, but the profession is only in its infancy, and it is obvious that a more elastic technique and greater versatility are called for. Many animals are nocturnal in their habits and, though this is also true of some babies, the pet-sitter may well find that her life is less sedentary than she expected. It is one thing to curl up with a good book beside a bowl of newts or a stertorous lapdog, quite another to spend an evening with an ape to whom you have only just been introduced or to make it possible for a snake charmer to attend his regimental reunion.

AUTHOR! AUTHOR!

Considering how invariably successful pantomimes always seem to be, and how much pleasure they give to large sections of the population in all parts of the country, it is strange that one hears so little of their authors. The curtain falls on the last splendid scene to a thunder—or anyhow to a brisk crepitation, for some of the clappers have small, sticky hands—of applause; but there are no cries of "Author!" nor, if there were, have any of us the slightest idea of what we should see if they were responded to. The talented creature or syndicate of creatures to whom we owe so much are impossible to visualize. The mind that can so effortlessly churn out such quantities of verse can be no ordinary mind; and the audacious mastery shown in mingling the sublime with the ridiculous, the sugary with the salty, has scarcely been paralleled since SHAKESPEARE'S day. MR. RATTIGAN, MR. USTINOV, MR. COWARD—they are very clever, of course, in their own ways; but none of their characters flies through the air or vanishes in puffs of smoke, and none of them has dared to interpolate between two passages of high romance a scene in which the protagonists throw buckets of whitewash over each other for no discoverable reason.

It can safely be said that no class of author is more indispensable than the pantomimographer. If (let us say) all the historians suddenly stopped writing history, or if some frightful form of paralysis put an end to the production of all modern poetry, it is to be feared that the vast majority of the population would be quite unaware of the loss to British culture; while not all of those who did realize what had happened would be equally distressed, and some might hardly be distressed at all. The only literary deprivation which really would come as a blow to the whole great soggy mass of the British public would be that caused by the people who write pantomimes ceasing to write them.

This makes it all the harder to explain, let alone to excuse, the studied neglect with which they are treated by the rest of the world. It is true that there is a certain basic lack of originality about the themes which they so opulently embroider; but a precisely similar weakness has never prevented SHAKESPEARE from being taken seriously, and it is really impossible to condone the scanty attention which the authors of pantomimes receive from the dramatic critics. " If Mr. A's *Jack and the Beanstalk* scarcely fulfils the dazzling promise of his *Mother Goose*, it is perhaps because the influence of Ibsen, faintly but excitingly discernible in the earlier work, here obtrudes itself too starkly, suppressing rather than evoking the Maeterlinckian *mystique* which is and must always be integral to the ambience of great folk-drama." Why do they never write about poor Mr. A. like this? If, instead of a pantomime in twenty-four magnificent scenes with a cast of a hundred, he had written a play in two acts with only three characters, and if this piece, instead of playing for weeks to crowded and enthusiastic houses, had been put on for a single ghastly performance on a Sunday evening, it is in these sort of terms that his talents would have been analysed. Poor Mr. A! Why is he never pointed out to one at literary parties (" He wrote *Little Red Riding Hood*, you know ")? Why is he never photographed for the society papers, brooding soulfully over a rhyming dictionary in his study or fingering his white tie in the foyer at a first night? The whole thing is inexplicable and rather sad.

" EXCLUSITIVITY "

It is—or, at least, it ought to be—one of the first principles of etymology that new words are only coined in response to new demands. The Word, in spite of all that poets and logical positivists tell us, exists for the Thing. In a legal document read in the Court of Appeal recently the expression " exclusitivity " occurred. " This is a new word to me," commented LORD JUSTICE BIRKETT to counsel, who replied—whether hopefully or merely helplessly the report fails to say—that it was " a word that might come into use." The learned counsel's subjunctive will ring ominously in purists' ears. It hints at an ultimate *laissez-faire* of language, at an unmentionable verbal anarchy in which every man becomes his own Webster and Roget's *Thesaurus* is capable of indefinite expansion. There is no aesthetic justification for " exclusitivity's " existence. It cannot simply have sprung out of some poet's head. It does not chime majestically like " Chimborazo." SIR THOMAS BROWNE would not have used it about his urns. DONNE would not have buried it like a nugget in a funeral sermon.

The nearest word to " exclusitivity " that exists at present is " exclusivism." It is, the *Oxford Dictionary* declares, " the principle or practice of being exclusive." Similarly, an exclusivist is " one who maintains the exclusive validity of a theory." Neither word is in frequent demand, though MR. GLADSTONE once made orotund use of the second in an article he wrote for the *Nineteenth Century*. " The field of Greek mythology," declared the Grand Old Man magisterially, " . . . is the sporting-ground of the exclusivists of the solar theory." This is helpful so far as it goes. Unfortunately, it does not go nearly far enough, since it fails to provide a reasonable basis for "exclusitivity's" existence. The dictionary approach is obviously the wrong one. A surer method of determining the meaning of the word is to compare it with other current neologisms. Here, fortunately, a parallel suggests itself at once. Two or three years ago "productivity" had as hard a battle to win acceptance as "exclusitivity" is having now. Even to-day its correct use is mainly restricted to economists. Who, apart from those grey figures, can safely say, with his hand on his heart, that he knows what "productivity" means? Yet in the popular mind the word has come to have a distinct "emotive" value. For most people it means no more than intensified production. Similarly, "exclusitivity" must obviously mean the quintessence of exclusiveness.

Used in this sense, its value becomes apparent at once. It is obviously a literary word, an expression evolved by novelists to convey shades of social awareness which have been hitherto unexpressed. Its value to literary men of all kinds must be indescribable. How greatly, once he had got over his first careless antipathy, its use would have smoothed the late CHARLES SCOTT-MONCRIEFF'S path while he was translating Proust. Though examples of "exclusitivity" in literature are innumerable, its greatest exponent was undoubtedly the Duke of Dorset. "Exclusitivity" was his Grace's religion and he found a perfect shrine for it in his management of that holy of holies, the Junta. When the Duke joined the club there were, SIR MAX BEERBOHM declares, four members. These all left Oxford at the end of the summer term and the Duke "inaugurated in solitude his second year of membership." From time to time he proposed and seconded other candidates, but always, when the last Tuesday of term drew near, he began to have his doubts.

After dinner, when the two club servants had placed on the mahogany the time-worn Candidates' Book and the ballot-box, and had noiselessly withdrawn, the Duke clearing his throat, read aloud to himself " Mr. So-and-So, of Such-and-Such College, proposed by the Duke of Dorset, seconded by the Duke of Dorset " and, in every case, when he drew out the drawer of the ballot-box, found it was a black ball that he had dropped into the urn. Learned counsel, if he is given to reading *Zuleika Dobson*, may well feel that " exclusitivity " can go no farther.

BOOKS AND BARONETS

Where the famous shades of literature gather on the asphodel one distinguished class must lately have displayed considerable interest. The baronets must have been glad to hear, albeit with a certain condescension, that four new members had been admitted to their order. Books are full of baronets and there is one of them whose normally languid sensations cannot have been so powerfully aroused for a long while. Sir Walter Elliot of Kellynch Hall, as we know, " for his own amusement never took up any book but the baronetage." Now, after a long interval, he can feel once more " pity and contempt " for new creations and with a renewed eagerness admiration for " the limited remnant of the earlier patents." MISS AUSTEN may claim the arch-baronet, but from the stables, if they may so be termed, of other eminent authors have come baronets of high quality. Sir Walter Elliot would have been seventeen when *The School for Scandal* was first acted and might well have gone up from Somerset to see it. How he would have revelled in its four baronets (they can none of them have been knights)—Sir Peter Teazle, Sir Oliver Surface, Sir Benjamin Backbite and Sir Harry Bumper. SHERIDAN must have adored baronets, for having begun with a mere two—Sir Anthony Absolute and Sir Lucius O'Trigger, he now created four and all of different kinds.

Baronets have a reputation for wickedness but some of the names that spring to mind hardly bear this out. There is Sir Leicester Dedlock, for instance, who " is only a baronet but there is no baronet mightier than he." He is not in the least wicked. Stupid, yes, but even so Laurence Boythorn ought not to have called him " the most coxcombical and utterly brainless ass." He was a gallant, obstinate, honourable, old gentleman. To be sure he was pompous, but baronets in literature rather run to pomposity. There are two good samples from SIR WALTER SCOTT's stable, Sir Arthur Wardour of Knockwinnock and Sir Robert Hazlewood of Hazlewood, who was puffed up by having recently inherited a Nova Scotia baronetcy. But if we want the best, whether in variety or splendour of title, we must go to THACKERAY. There is no name so appropriate and sonorous as that of Sir Pitt Crawley, for nearly all the best baronets are christened by surnames. He was a disreputable old scamp and doubtless Sir Huddlestone Fuddlestone and Sir Giles Wapshot found him a trying neighbour; but he was far superior to the miserable, twittering little wretch, Sir Francis Clavering. And then, if we want real villainy there never was a meaner and more hateful scoundrel than Sir Barnes Newcome. In villainy DICKENS could do no better than Sir Mulberry Hawk—a fine name but a character purely of the theatre and the transpontine theatre at that. WILKIE COLLINS was not amiss with Sir Percival Glyde, who never would have been a baronet if he had not forged an entry in the marriage register. But already this random list grows too long and might go on almost for ever. "He might have been a peer if he had played his cards better," said Lord Steyne of the late Sir Pitt Crawley. Thank goodness he did not; we should have missed the noblest baronet of them all.

TIME OVER AGAIN

Tinker, tailor, soldier, sailor—still the children murmur the old incantation as they count the prune stones that remain on holiday plates no longer made exciting at pudding time by mince pies. Still, after that generally accepted beginning, disputes arise over the variant readings that may finish a peep into the future. Gentleman, apothecary, ploughboy, thief are the only possible words for some, but not for all. Rich man, poor man, beggar man, thief is authentic necromancy in many nurseries. A critic with his ears open as dinner draws to its close will note that the text, orally handed down, has been got at by modern invention. Soldier brave, sailor true, skilled physician, Oxford blue, portly rector, squire so hale, dashing airman, curate pale—when did that dashing airman come in? Did he not, unless memory fails, take the place of an outmoded type, the haughty huntsman? A boy, having arrived by one of these routes at foreknowledge of his profession and a girl at what her husband is going to be, proceed to fix the date. This year, next year, sometime, never—how often do stones run out on the last word, and how little this depressing negative dismays youth. "Never" is a word that means nothing to a child.

For grown ups watching the little victims play, "never" means only too much. They can no longer look forward to becoming Oxford blues or skilled physicians. They have, most of them, had quite enough of being soldiers, sailors, or airmen. The reflection that a man is in a groove arises as often at the New Year as does the wish to be able to make and keep resolutions. A common bond between men of almost all professions is that, if they could put back the clock, they would take up some other aid to solvency. There are exceptions to this rule. Actors, judging by their reminiscences, seem to be ecstatically content with their walk of life. Genius in any art is a compelling tyrant that leaves its chosen without a choice. The ruck, in business and in medicine, in the services and at the bar, looks enviously over the other man's fence. " If I had my time over again " say nine men out of ten, and then go on to wish for a change and to vow that their sons shall not follow in the ill-rewarded drudgery of their footsteps.

HORACE, who was more often than not right, suggests that, if some god granted their prayers, letting the soldier turn trader and the lawyer go on the land, they would all refuse, and he may be right, but the rest of his argument is more doubtful. Discontent with the job in hand derives, in his view, from greed. The truth is surely that it has its roots in romance and in rebellion against the limitations of mind and body. A man who is so clumsy with his fingers that he cannot tie a parcel that will not come adrift in the post office may still dream of his name (had the prune stones arranged themselves more justly) appearing high in an Honours List as reward for his eminence as a surgeon. Realism may teach him that it is only for children that the sky is the limit. Even then, he can cherish two almost universal adult illusions. He can picture himself happy, far away from town, as a farmer and, as LORD BURNHAM pointed out the other day, he will have no doubts but that he could edit a newspaper.

ON WITH THE MOTLEY!

To masquerade is in our language a verb with equivocal connotations; it suggests a slightly frivolous and definitely unsuccessful imposture. The truth of the matter is that as a nation we do not really approve of what—with a characteristic note of disdain—we call fancy dress. It is all very well for foreigners to go capering about in dominoes; they like that sort of thing. We do not. At the cry of "On with the motley!" the average Englishman's blood runs cold. He asks himself, if he is a thoughtful fellow, how it is that this canker has never been eradicated from our social life. Perhaps Britannia, perched on a rock in that ridiculous get-up, or John Bull, with his frightful waistcoat, have somehow sanctified the addiction to dressing up of a small but active section of the population. Whatever the cause, fancy dress remains, if not a British institution, a sort of minor epidemic which is constantly breaking out and from which only a few hardy islanders have achieved complete immunity.

The ladies, though they often complain bitterly, are generally thought to suffer less than the gentlemen by being compelled to dress up, since this is an activity to which, in a modified form, they devote most of their lives anyhow. Besides, they do not have to park the car, a duty of which gentlemen should never be unmindful in selecting their costume; nothing is more calculated to impair self-confidence than to walk along a rain-swept public thoroughfare in the character of an Ancient Briton. Some gentlemen, traitors to their sex, throw themselves with enthusiasm into the business of dressing up. Their aim is generally either to impress or to divert, and it may in general be said that a reveller who pursues the latter object and comes as the Spirit of Austerity or the

Abominable Snowman is regarded with more tolerance than the exquisite in a perruque and patches.

The great ruck of malcontents aim chiefly at comfort of mind and body. The latter is best achieved by a purely perfunctory disguise, but for the sake of the former it must not be too perfunctory; nothing, when the time comes, is more boring than constantly having to answer the question "What are you supposed to be?" Among points unlikely to be overlooked by the experienced masquerader are the importance of pockets, the folly of wigs, and the undesirability of wearing any form of helmet. Costumes depending for their effect on cumbrous accessories should be avoided; to set out for the ball burdened with a lifebelt, a stuffed goshawk, a scythe, a croquet mallet, or a rickshaw is only less ill advised than to allow your partner to equip herself with (and eventually ask you to take charge of) a shepherdess's crook, a tambourine, a wheatsheaf, a butterfly net, or a basket of imitation fruit. These caveats indicate only a few of the perils and inconveniences of masquerade, and it is easy to understand why most decent Englishmen infinitely prefer putting on a scarlet coat, black trousers, and a stiff white shirt for the Hunt Ball to donning some garish and uncomfortable outfit and going to a fancy dress dance.

UNFAIR TO POPINJAYS

The lifting to-day of the ban on parrots from oversea should not be greeted too readily as a cause for rejoicing among those much-wronged birds. They may have welcomed the order, made twenty-one years ago, which denied them the hospitality of British cages. It was a resounding order applied to the whole family and covering parrakeets, lovebirds, macaws, cockatoos, cockatiels, conures, caiques, lories, and lorikeets. Now that their susceptibility to psittacosis has been found to be shared by seagulls, ducks, turkeys, and other birds and that the disease has been robbed of most of its dangers, another parrot invasion is imminent. The veterans, who have been holding the fort, can look forward to young reinforcements.

If the tales of sailormen are to be believed, some stray immigrants have successfully run the gauntlet of the customs. A doped bird has been slipped inside trousers legs. A ship's cat has been carried in a basket for an airing ashore by the last man off, who has protested that, if he opened up, the animal would run back on deck. Authority proving sceptical, the lid has been lifted and the cat duly seen to disappear in the direction of the galley. After pursuit, the aggrieved owner of the basket would make a second attempt to pass and be allowed to do so unchecked, and this time with a cargo of parrots. Such nefarious transactions, if they were ever undertaken, need be stooped to no longer. Gay plumage can be flaunted among the baggage on the counter and ready tongues taught to repeat that they have nothing to declare.

What, if they could find their own words, would they have to say about this renewed freedom to enter comfortable prisons? They might reproach their hosts for

G—2

having taken away from them their proud old name of " popinjay " and applied it to a silly section of humanity. They might protest against the miscellany of libels of which they are victims. Scarcely a year passes but one of them is accused of having waited for at least a hundred years before laying its first egg. Their alleged aptitude for swearing is so notorious that one of them should learn to quote Caliban's " You taught me language; and my profit on't is, I know how to curse." The generations of parrots that have been honoured residents in the most respectable society have failed to wipe out this slur. Nor have the no less numerous birds who used their beaks on nothing but seed wiped out the memory of a vicious few who are as much in a minority as are dogs that bite strangers or men who start a fight in a bar parlour. Now that the grey bird with the red tail and his fellows are coming back, they deserve to be received with imaginative sympathy. Accustomed to noisy company and bright skies at home, they may find a cage as little congenial as do more obviously restless captives. It will be a poor reception for them if the most the British can say in self defence is that at least they do not, as some people have done in the past, esteem parrots as a table delicacy.

BLACK INTO WHITE

In the good old days, when history was history and consisted of dates and facts to be learnt by heart, one of the best established facts was that kings were either black or white. They were trumps or the most worthless of low cards. The former were wise, manly, and strong, and the latter weak, self-indulgent, under the thumbs of favourites, always getting beaten by the Scots and French and by their own barons, running into debt and ending up, in many cases, as victims of a sensational murder. Lately, there has been a steady, scholarly swing—disturbing to those whose history stays rooted in tradition—towards finding good in bad kings.

JOHN, who glowered from the pages of the old text books as menacingly as he does at Madame Tussaud's, turns out to have done a lot for the Navy. That was the prerogative of the impeccable ALFRED until, under the new fashion, it was shared by JAMES II. JOHN, it seems, was not only a sailor king. He had intellectual tastes, made a collection of theological and classical books, and was so fond of reading that, at the height of a political crisis in England, he could not bear to be separated from his library and had it shipped over from Normandy. WILLIAM RUFUS, into whose eye an arrow was steered by providential accident, might be thought to be proof against kindness to kings. Now, it seems that he was a man of action who once left the hunting field on a sudden call and, in spite of the protests of his companions, crossed the Channel in a gale and saved the situation. What is worse, that " accident " in a hunting field that he did not leave may well have been a deliberate plot in which his brother HENRY, who was among those present in the New Forest, appears only too likely to have been involved.

This same HENRY, formerly so secure among the good, and admiringly called BEAUCLERC, proves to have had " at least " twenty children, of whom only two were born in lawful wedlock.

After this the connoisseur of black and white has little fight left in him. He is prepared to agree that, as he has lately been told, RICHARD II was a talented administrator. He gives up, without a murmur of protest, the attractive crook-backed villainy of RICHARD III and accepts him as the founder of the post office. He ceases to raise his eyebrows in disdain at the coarse behaviour of a fat figure of fun known as PRINNY and, instead, admires the cleverness and the good taste in architecture and painting of GEORGE IV. Having been brought up to slander GEORGE III as an aged lunatic who thought SHAKESPEARE sorry stuff, he accepts the fair and friendly portrait of him sketched, yesterday, by MR. I. R. CHRISTIE in a public lecture at University College, London. The George who, in middle age, rode forty miles before beginning the day's work and, spurning his coach, walked twelve of the miles from Windsor to London, deserved, as MR. CHRISTIE claims, the respect of sedentary caricaturists. Who knows but that one day EDWARD II will be discovered to have won a strategic victory at Bannockburn ?

HOMING CATS

Yet another cat has just walked home by himself across unknown country. It was a comparatively unadventurous performance, involving no more than a stroll of forty miles from Birmingham, a city to which the animal had apparently taken a dislike, to the more congenial neighbourhood of Banbury. Examples of this feline accomplishment in pathfinding are so commonly reported that there seems no scientific reason to doubt that cats have a mysterious sense of direction. Bonzo, a lady who lived, shortly before the war, at Exmouth, was taken with her kitten, in a basket and in a car, for the seventy-three-mile ride to Bodmin. Life across the Cornish border did not suit her, but being a good mother she put up with exile until the kitten could look after itself, and then hiked home over Bodmin Moor, the outskirts of Dartmoor, and thence either through Exeter or down the by-pass and over the Exe at Countess Weir Bridge. When she reported for home duties again, she paraded with pads quite firm, coat shiny, almost fat and in excellent morale. A Cockney cat of an earlier generation, whose exploit was never recorded in print, similarly found his way for some miles through London traffic.

These migrants belong to an impressive bevy of travelling cats. Their methods deserve systematic study, which appears hitherto to have been neglected. The naturalist who undertakes what would be a generally interesting piece of field work must consider other evidence of the cats' power of discrimination. How did the ship's cat who once belonged to—or, as he no doubt thought, owned—the White Star liner Adriatic recognize the blast of her siren? She had, unpardonably, sailed from Liverpool without him. Puss prowled in irritation about the

Gladstone dock for three weeks, and on hearing the hoot of his wandering home as it returned to port, he grew so excited that he could scarcely wait for the gangway to be made fast. How he knew one ship's noise from another is as hard to explain as is the impulse that led a kitten, in a recent summer, to cross the Matterhorn, and another kitten, of some twenty years ago, to go mountaineering in the Bernese Oberland and, on being kidnapped and brought down in a rucksack, to escape and repeat its Excelsior act.

How to set about scientifically explaining this instinct which leads cats sometimes to take a bee-line for home, and at others to " go places " may take a little working out. It would be easy to ring cats and to enlarge them at varying distances from home, but they would resent being turned into *ex officio* birds, and a disgruntled cat can be terribly uncooperative. The chances are that, subjected to such indignity, they would choose a spot exposed to the east wind and curl up there as comfortably as though they were back by the familiar saucer and fireside. It would only be after the observer had caught cold that they would deign to move. Besides, even if they were prepared to play the ringing game, little would be proved, except what is already known, that a cat has its private method of navigation. Here is a challenge to the scientists who have, so far, failed to get much change out of the migratory habits of birds. At least a cat—thank goodness—is wingless and so more easy to keep an eye on. Its prowess overland invites investigation, for in spite of the horse that found its way unaided from Dublin to Kildare, and of all manner of tall stories about dogs, cats may claim to hold the four-footed record for cryptic map reading.

LI PO IN THE RED SQUARE

Those whose literary snobbery is not so great as to preclude their reading verse in translation have long derived enjoyment and instruction from Chinese poetry. Through the urbane medium of an Arthur Waley or a Soame Jenyns they have been introduced to a strange and picturesque world of the imagination—a world of peach blossom and blue hills, of princesses idling in jade pavilions and clouds moving for a thousand *li* over snow-capped peaks thickly populated with hermits. The gibbons chatter by the Great Wall, the solitaries fill themselves with the Tao, the erudite and slightly fuddled Civil servants launch their cups of wine upon the artificial lake. Disgraced mandarins, condemned to a lifetime of tax-collecting in remote frontier posts, mourn the scholarly pleasures of Peking. The ghosts of great courtesans, the spirits of grave ancestors, speak of the mutability of fortune. Ageing courtiers lament the *douceur de vivre* that once reigned in the courtyards of the Summer Palace. " The actors in the pear garden have aged," they tell us, " the eunuchs in the pepper room have lost their charm."

Alas, that willow-patterned life is to-day as dead as the Empress Dowager. It has vanished with the rest of the old-world China that we knew, with Kai Lung and the Swineherd Hoti, with Goldsmith's Citizen of the World and Signor Varé's Temple of Costly Experience. It is as obsolete as the Twentyish cult for mah-jong and dragon-embroidered dressing-gowns. The Chinese poet of to-day is a tougher, coarser-fibred creature. Conditioned by the spirit of the age, he has become a political animal. That, at least, is the conclusion to which one is regretfully driven by reports of a recent " Chinese Literary Evening " held in the Moscow Conservatoire. The conversazione, so a Peking broadcast informs us, was attended by 2,000 Russian writers, scientists, artists, students, and Stakhanovites. (The presence of this last-named mercurial class, doubtless wearing the emblems of their Pindaric feats with tractor or conveyor-belt, will ring reassuringly in the ears of those who might otherwise fear the deviationist nature of the gathering.)

Headed by the chief of their delegation, MR. TING-LING, the poets read to the company from their works. Tributes to MR. STALIN predominated and MR. TING-LING himself read a poem entitled " Evening in Red Square." This at least suggests the note of wistful elegy that one associates with the spiritual heirs of LI PO and PO CHÜ-I. Yet there is something incongruous in the idea of these olive-skinned and fastidious literary men solemnly tempering their ditties to the husky flute of ideology. The Chinese poet of to-day has no time to climb Omeî Shan, to watch the wild geese flying south in the tenth month or to listen to the orioles calling to each other among the maple trees upon the banks of the Yangtze. One day he may be able to do these things, but to-day, as MR. AUDEN once remarked, " To-day the Struggle ! "

A NOBLE CLOCK

Other great timepieces are older or more weighty than Big Ben, but none of them compares with him for world fame, and the news that he is about to be silent for some hours, while his hammer work is overhauled, will spread far and wide. When members of Parliament were hovering, like anxious fairies, over his birth, they were reassured by the CHIEF LORD of the WOODS and FORESTS (now called, prosaically, Minister of Works) that this child of the craftsman's art would grow up to be " a Noble Clock, indeed a King of Clocks, the biggest and best in the world, within sight and sound of the heart of London." Seldom has an official prophecy come more nearly true. Great Paul is heavier by a few tons, Great Peter of York is nearly as heavy, and comparative lightweights—such as the Great Toms of Oxford and Lincoln—have historic claims that they may be unprepared to waive for any metropolitan rival. Big Ben, silent or sounding, shining in the dark or unlit (as he briefly was in a recent fuel crisis), remains in prestige the great grandfather of all clocks. Always keeping a keen eye on the march of time, he was quick to see the importance of the wireless to a public figure and, as early as 1923, he made his first broadcast.

Although he is a Victorian, he inherited an older tradition. The Clock Tower is said to have risen after a medieval Lord Chief Justice, who falsified a court record, had been fined and the money used to erect a bell striking the hours and reminding the judges in Westminster Hall indifferently to administer justice. A more scientific duty was, from the first, assigned to the unborn Big Ben. He must, demanded the then Astronomer Royal of startled clockmakers, register the time correct to one second a day by the first stroke of the hour bell and the record of his performance should be telegraphed twice daily to Greenwich Observatory. When all seemed ready, the long heralded clock took up his position—and while London laughed—he refused to go. The generation of scoffers departed out of earshot of Big Ben and an Astronomer Royal in our own day set the seal on his excellence. The late SIR FRANK DYSON reported that, in one year, the greatest error had been only slightly more than a second and that on only twenty-one days had it even passed the second mark.

This remarkable accuracy has been safeguarded by a no less notable device. A tray was fixed half way down the pendulum and, when time lagged ever so slightly, a halfpenny or penny was placed on the tray. The pendulum then moved a shade more quickly and, so, gradually brought the clock back to time. Impatience, leading to a gain, was corrected by removing the coin. It is well to recall such ingenuities, by which Big Ben has kept his proud record, for whenever, however mildly, he is in trouble he cannot hope to keep quiet about it. The starlings, those London street urchins on wings, squatted impudently on his hands a year or so ago and made him late by the unheard of stretch of five minutes. Some time before a wrongly placed painter's ladder got him with equal prominence into the news. The silence that is to come upon him for a few hours to-morrow is nothing to worry about. Those who look up to him every time they pass through Parliament Square and the many millions more who set their watches by his voice over the air need not be anxious. Their old friend in war and peace will continue to keep them punctual.

GONGS

Not all of us are music-lovers, and even those who are do not love all forms of music. A century or so ago a cultured European lady, hearing the bagpipes for the first time, stoically noted in her *carnets de voyage*, " We must be thankful that they do not also smell." The ululations of the saxophone are apt to send shudders down the spine of devout opera-goers, and in many of us there resides a deep indifference to the harp. But there is, or rather there used to be, one musical instrument whose sound made an equal and an instantaneous appeal to the tone-deaf, the jazz-mad, and the Wagnerian. It came from Malaya, " but is now " (said the dictionary in 1901 and again in 1933) " very generally employed in European countries as an instrument of call, esp. to summon a household to meals." Well, we still have households and we still, in a manner of speaking, have meals ; but very few of us now have gongs. No longer, conjured by the butler's flawless wristwork, does that crescendo of sound—so urbane, so portentous, so welcome—march irresistibly up staircases, fan out into the bachelors' wing, flood across the lawns down to the tennis courts, sounding its punctual clarion to the gastric juices. No such majestic summons to meals is heard to-day. The words " It's in," spoken with a strong undercurrent of apprehension and uncertainty, make a poor substitute.

There may be a few houses where the gong, perhaps even the dressing-gong, is still heard—houses where the gong-stick (or whatever that civilized little club is called) has to be hung up out of reach of small children, from whom there is always danger of false and deafening alarms. But such establishments cannot be numerous. Vast strides have been made in methods of intercommunication, but the gong (than which no more economical or expeditious method of conveying intelligence was ever devised) has fallen into untimely obsolescence. What, one cannot help speculating, has happened to all these instruments of call, these valuable disks usually (according to the dictionary) made of four parts copper to one of tin ? Were they, during the war which so few of them seem to have survived, converted into Spitfires, or turned over to the Home Guard as frying pans or perhaps even as shields ? Would a modern child, if he found one suspended from its stand in the box-room, know what it was, or had been, for ?

These are difficult questions to answer. What is certain is that the gong, which " falls like thunder on the dizzy ear "—SOUTHEY's butler had perhaps been having a row with the cook—is now rarely heard in our islands. It may be that, in some of the larger Ministries, its notes—probably in triplicate—periodically announce the tea-interval ; but in general it would seem that we have outgrown the gong—or rather, to be accurate, that the gong, which belonged to a more spacious life, has outgrown us. The accents in which, in bygone days, people used to remark " The gong has gone " ranged from the complacent to the flurried ; now we can only say the words wistfully.

JULIET STANDS FOR J.

If we are to emulate—and it is pretty generally agreed that we should have a bash at it—the earlier Elizabethans, we must seek to cultivate their attitude of mind towards fundamentals; and we shall not make much progress until we start treating the alphabet (than which, after all, few things are more fundamental) in the tough yet insouciant manner adopted towards it by those of GOOD QUEEN BESS's subjects who knew what it was. The achievement of widespread illiteracy is not perhaps a cause to which as a nation we could whole-heartedly dedicate ourselves to-day; and our ancestors' methods of spelling, so admirably flexible and opportunist, might if we attempted to recapture them excite the ridicule of our neighbours, who would soon be in two minds as to whether we were the Brittysshe or the Brytishe people.

What is principally needed is a reassertion of the principle that the letters of the alphabet are, as they were in Elizabethan days, a medium for written and not for oral communication. SIR WALTER RALEIGH would never have referred to his motherland as the U.K., even had it been historically sound for him to do so. Letters were seen and not heard, and the citizens did not live in the perplexing shadow of organizations and dignitaries whose designations could be invoked only by pronouncing the sort of un-word so painfully familiar to the less successful type of crossword-puzzle addict—NKVD, ECA, BGS, TUC, UNESCO, SNOIC. This form of tyranny, under which the neo-Elizabethans live without serious or effective complaint, has latterly been accompanied by a yet more striking example of our subservience to the alphabet. Not content with fashioning formless totems out of groups of letters, we now feel obliged—in specialized but important contexts—to rename the letters of the alphabet, giving to each a whole word by which, whenever it is heard and not seen, it is entitled to, and indeed must, be known.

It started in a small way, with acks and tocs and pips and emmas. But, with the growing military use of telephones and radio-telephones, these comparatively inoffensive little equivalents were found (one supposes) to be insufficiently distinctive and were replaced by a new and more elaborate régime. Many a keen young recruit to the infantry must spend his first night at the regimental depôt in a state of terrible suspense. His dearest hope is to be posted to Able Company, with its atmosphere of spruce, almost effortless efficiency. But he well knows that the odds are against him, that he is more likely to find himself in the *petit bourgeois* ambience of Baker Company, or among the vulgar camaraderie of Charlie, the indefinable degeneracy of Dog or the sickly hedonism of Sugar.

It would be bad enough if the letters were only given their names on active service; but they have them in civilian life as well, and with three or four exceptions (the irrepressible Charlie being one) they are different names. Q, which to a tank commander can only be Queen, becomes Queenie on the softer lips of the telephone operator; Baker acquires Benjamin on demobilization. Item becomes Isaac, and Fox is scarcely recognizable as Frederick. The situation is further complicated by survivors of the old régime—nobody calls a soldier on a motor-bicycle a Dog Roger—and as if all this pluralistic confusion were not enough there has lately been an attempt to introduce an international ABC for the use of pilots and radio officers. In this Baker (or Benjamin) must be called Bravo, Roger turns into Romeo, and Juliet stands for J (instead of the other way round). But it almost seems as if, at last, a halt is being called to the seemingly endless business of naming and renaming letters, for it is reported that the newest alphabet is unpopular and is being little used. If this is true, it is Oboe King by us.

DRAMA IN THE COURTS

The death of SIR PATRICK HASTINGS removes one of those famous advocates who, in every generation, heighten the dramatic interest of the law courts. Laymen, unable to follow the intricacy of Chancery proceedings, are rapt readers and spectators of a criminal trial. This sometimes brings on them the reproach of indulging an unhealthy taste for murder and other seamy sides of life, but the spell cast by Judge and counsel may fairly be described as aesthetic. A not unpleasant reaction of horror is, indisputably, included in it. " You have conducted many hundreds of post-mortem examinations ? " asks an Attorney-General, and SIR BERNARD SPILSBURY corrects him with " many thousands." That—there can be no denying—sends a shiver down the spine of citizens whom fate has spared contact with violence. They are held, too, by the factor of doubt and the excitement of detection which have entered into all the memorable trials for murder. It was not the sordid background but the tensity of the dialogue that made so memorable that interjection by MR. JUSTICE DARLING of " One moment, Major Armstrong ! " That was an example of how the atmosphere of drama affects even the Bench, for the Judge, aided by his gentle voice, purposefully put down his pen and leaned forward, before he began his twenty minutes of questions about the dandelion-killing experiment.

LORD AVORY—that great criminal advocate and Judge—was a favourite actor who never played to the gallery. A witness aptly summed his reputation up when, in answer to the warning that, if he went on, he would make the Judge angry, he said, " In that event, my Lord, I shall have achieved something." At the opposite extreme was Bottomley who delighted his public by conducting his own cases—which, as a rule, he richly deserved to lose—against the champion heavy-weights at the Bar. Cases that may be described as having played to crowded houses are as diverse as the actors. Marshall-Hall defending in the " Brides in the Bath " case, the colossal vanity of Patrick Mahon, and the ugly echo of the Charing Cross trunk murder come into the category of melodrama. Light comedy is achieved when Darling puts an easel beside him on the Bench, fills the jury box with artists (appearing not as jurymen but as witnesses) and sets the reporters questing through books of quotation to verify his literary allusions.

Audiences can be fickle. They cheered Sievier when, with Rufus Isaacs defending him, he was acquitted of attempting to obtain money by menaces and they chuckled over his subsequent conviction on another charge with his former counsel now his Judge. Above all, they look for individuality. The brogue that could be agreeable as the Blarney Stone and as menacing as the black cap on the Judge's wig helped Carson. The mixture of an explosive kind of common sense and a talent for picturesque exaggeration with a tendency to fling down his papers and stalk out of Court made Marshall-Hall a star among legal actors. For the moment there seems to be a lull in these dramatized variations on the cool progress of the Courts. Bench and Bar may have adopted the matter-of-fact fashion of Members of Parliament, who, with few exceptions, avoid rhetoric. If so, it is not because public taste has changed. An exciting case tried and argued dramatically will always draw.

TARZAN TARZANOVITCH

" Placing his foot upon the body of his kill, he uttered the reverberating cry of the bull ape." It was thus, if childhood memories are not at fault, that Tarzan was wont to signalize the successive proofs of his prowess. It struck one at the time as slightly ostentatious, but one realized that Tarzan knew no better and after all he generally had done something pretty good, like turning an alligator inside out or throwing a buffalo over a cliff. But of all his feats none is better worth reverberating over than his latest; he has got past the Iron Curtain. It is true that Russian audiences are not being allowed to swallow him neat; the films in which he appears are preceded by a foreword which " explains that Tarzan is the child of a rich Englishman, raised in innocence by the jungle apes, and that he never encountered the corrupting influence of bourgeois culture till he met American explorers."

The first of these two statements is, of course, historically correct. The fact that Tarzan's father was an English nobleman (Earl Greystoke) is too often forgotten, and nobody in Hollywood, most regrettably, has ever taken the opportunity of making a film called *Tarzan in the House of Lords* (" See the mighty ape-man swinging from chandelier to chandelier in Britain's historic legislature ! See him rout the famed corps of Beefeaters on the battlements of Big Ben while all London watches spellbound !"). As for the corrupting influence of bourgeois culture, one cannot help feeling that the Russian authorities ought, in their own interests, to have been rather more specific. Compared with most heroes of American films, Tarzan seems singularly immune from the dread effects of bourgeois culture. He does not wear a top hat, go to night-clubs, own a yacht, drink, gamble or even read the wrong sort of books. He is, it is true, an individualist, but he cannot very well help that, since there is, as it were, only one of him. His failure to realize that all American explorers are, *ex officio*, Imperialist spies must tell against him to some extent; but otherwise it is not easy to recall any outstanding symptoms of Western degeneracy.

It would really be more satisfactory if the Russians got down to it and started making their own Tarzan films. In these the protagonist would be a less isolated figure; the ends of doctrine might best be served by making him the chairman of a small committee of apemen and apewomen, organized on collective lines and marked by a tendency to go in for useful things like irrigation schemes instead of frittering away their energies wrestling with rhinoceroses. In the end, no doubt, the explorers—Russian explorers—would turn up, and for the first time Tarzan and his colleagues would learn of the existence of the U.S.S.R., a piece of intelligence which might well cause their chairman to utter the reverberating cry of the bull ape. Off they would all set for that bounteous and happy land, and outside their deserted huts we should see, to soft music, the baboons gazing in reverent awe at a life-size portrait of ——. But perhaps it would not be fair to give away the *dénouement*.

WEDDINGS ON WAX

A church in Australia, having installed the necessary apparatus, is to present each couple who get married there with a record of the ceremony. The project is a pleasing one, but perhaps it is time to examine the trend of which it is symptomatic. There was an epoch, far away in the mists of prehistory, when men and women progressed from the cradle to the grave without leaving behind them any very circumstantial evidence that they had done so. Another notch on somebody else's club perhaps signalized their arrival at their destination, and sometimes their fall into complete oblivion was partially broken by the rather impersonal tools and utensils which they took with them on the first stage of their journey into the unknown. But on the whole they left behind them only the very faintest of spoors. That, no doubt, is one of the main reasons why we allude to them as prehistoric.

Since then the human race, as though to offset the great strides it has made in improving its capacity to obliterate itself, has been at pains to impress ever deeper and more sharply defined footprints upon the sands of time. The invention of writing enabled those who had mastered this art to bequeath some sort of record to posterity; the invention of printing enlarged the scale of this bequest; and in a similar way photography placed a penny plain immortality within the reach of those who could not afford to sit, twopence coloured, for an Old Master. The scope for all this sort of thing has increased enormously within recent years. Not only does the State require the individual to furnish it, over and over again, with every conceivable particular about his personality and career, but the individual himself is tempted on all sides to avail himself of pictorial and other methods of making his own entries in the great herd-book of the human race.

Gone is the brackish photograph of the naked infant upon the horse-hair rug. Its place has been taken by several hundred feet of cinematograph film, upon which the first unsteady steps of the toddler are followed, not less unsteadily and for much too long, by the parental lens. The camera, once discharged with the sparing precision of a sniper's rifle, now clicks with the carefree prodigality of a Bren gun. The recording machine preserves the intonations of our voice, and artists are eager to execute a likeness of our dog. Now we can get our wedding on wax and hear again, as often as we desire, our voice, strangled or stentorian, utter the momentous words "I will." Our children, presumably, will be able to listen to themselves being christened, to us being buried. In many ways it is all very convenient; in one it is not. Where does one keep all this stuff? True, it does not take up so much space as a collection of family portraits; but it takes up some, and its requirements (which really include some sort of filing system) continually increase. As he rummages among the circumstantial but disorderly evidence of his existence, the contemporary citizen may well wish that he had settled, like some of his ancestors, for one really good equestrian statue and a couple of mentions in Pepys.

SIR OR MISTER

A nice little point in friendly Anglo-American relations has been raised over the correct way to address a stranger across the Atlantic. If an Englishman writes to a man whom he has never met, he generally begins " Dear Sir," but an American prefers " Dear Mr. So and So." Should either of them, knowing the other's convention, follow it in beginning a correspondence and, if he does not, which form should be taken in reply? May the writer who, so to speak, serves and plays by his own local rule, fairly expect the striker politely to copy him when the epistolary ball is returned? It is the sort of choice in which the English have had much practice, for they, more than any other people, complicate and enliven their lives with niceties of formal and informal style on paper and in conversation. The permutations of peroration in their letters run from " Yours faithfully " to " truly," " very truly," " sincerely," " yours ever," and plain " yours."

Italian has been described by a doughty linguist as the hardest language for a foreigner to talk idiomatically because of its wealth of synonyms and its endless changes of fashionable phrase. This may be so, but English surely leads in the strength of its serried ranks of titles and ways of verbal and written address. Frenchmen call their generals, but not their admirals, " my." Englishmen counter with confusion over a naval captain who may be referred to by rank alone and an army captain who must have his name sounded. Having met that challenge, they go on to score tricks with " Esq.," which involves the use of initials that are so often illegible, and with decorations which, in Government offices and other places where the " p's " and " q's " have to be minded, are scrupulously inserted from " G " to " K " and from " O " to " M " after titled or untitled names. Some of these pitfalls entrap the natives themselves. Is every true Briton sure in his choice between red, scarlet, and pink for the uniform of the hunting field ? Did not a bishop once see the letter he had signed " William Barchester " quoted from with the preliminary words " Mr. William writes from Barchester " ?

A judge is a more powerful piece than a bishop in this variety of chess. The law, even leaving out the moves permissible by Scottish judicial lords and colonial judges, has a series of masterly gambits. From the simple " Your Worship " of the magistrate's and " Your Honour " of the county court, the game progresses in interest. A puisne judge is addressed as a Lord when he is—if the expression be not contempt—" on the job," but he is not a Lord on an envelope. There he is " The Hon. Mr. Justice." As he is a knight, he is also " Sir ——," unless, like the late LORD RUSSELL of KILLOWEN, he has declined the honour. His brethren in the Court of Appeal are also their lordships on the bench, but are still not so in every-day life. There, one of their status is a " Right Honourable Lord Justice," a knight and a Privy Councillor, but he is not a life peer. That eminence is reserved for the Lords of Appeal in Ordinary. Contemplation of this Byzantine hierarchy reduces the decision to write to the man in New York as " Dear Sir " or by his name to a trifle to be settled by the toss of a coin.

BLESSINGS AND DISGUISES

Less attention than it merits would seem to have been attracted by a Press notice issued this month from the Secretaries' Office, H.M. Customs and Excise. Its matter is commendably free from sensationalism and its style from any striving after effect ; yet it is safe to say that no person of sensibility can read it without feeling at once humbled and uplifted. In simple, dignified language it reports that the Commissioners of Customs and Excise have been reviewing the liability to purchase tax of false beards and moustaches, and it goes on to announce their decisions in this matter. These—democratically arrived at " after consultation with the Trade "—are that false beards and moustaches " which are of a kind commonly sold as carnival goods (*e.g.*, moustaches designed to be clipped to the nose) and which are made up of bundles of natural or imitation hair glued to a backing or roughly twisted into the shape of a beard or moustache " will be liable to purchase tax. Henceforth, on the other hand, " theatrical beards and moustaches, each hair of which is separately waved or shaped and separately threaded to a backing designed to be gummed to the face, will be regarded as outside the scope of the tax."

In a planned economy, especially one as precarious as ours, any relaxation of controls must be looked at askance, and there may be some who will interpret the second of the Commissioners' decisions as the thin edge of a dangerous wedge, the first step in a Gadarene stampede down the slopes of *laissez faire* into the cruel sea of national ruin. To the average man, however, the action which the Commissioners have taken will seem judicious and enlightened. It is, in the average man's view, only just that the type of citizen who contemplates clipping to his nose a bundle of hair (whether natural or imitation) which has been roughly—contemptuously, almost—twisted into the shape of a moustache should be made to pay heavily for this insensate whim ; and, conversely, the Commissioners would have been doing a grave disservice to British culture if they had continued to impose a swingeing impost on articles without at least one of which no production of *King Lear* can hope to achieve the requisite standard of verisimilitude.

In spite of—or perhaps because of—his warm approval of what the Commissioners have done, the average man cannot help wishing that he knew a little more about how they did it. Those consultations with the Trade, for instance—what exactly happened when they took place ? Were the eminent perruquiers who attended them able to conceal their contempt for the retailers of what are " commonly sold as carnival goods " ? Was the junior Commissioner present, amid good-natured badinage, obliged to clip a specimen moustache to his nose ? Whose idea was the whole thing, anyway ? These are questions which, one fears, will never be answered. But at least the public have been vouchsafed a glimpse of a great bureaucracy at work upon fiscal reform, and it is a glimpse for which we must all feel grateful—especially, of course, those of us whose interests lie in the fields of either historical drama or espionage.

PER ARDUA AD OVA

It is by some reluctantly admitted, by others stoutly proclaimed, but by all generally agreed that what it is fashionable to call incentives act as a stimulant to most forms of human activity. We stand now on the threshold of a season when (as the old-fashioned bird-books used to put it) " nidification sets in," a development which, if precedent is anything to go by. will cause a sharp upward trend in the graphs devotedly kept by whichever Ministry has the duty of recording the frequency with which HER MAJESTY'S subjects climb trees. To many thoughtful persons it seems illogical that the Government, which insists that the citizen shall obtain a licence before he fells a tree and offers him a subsidy if he plants one, should seek neither to curb nor to further his ambitions to climb up one. For Darwinians allege that the citizen's remotest ancestors did very little else ; and the practice, having regard to the state of the world to-day, would not seem from a long-term point of view to have been conducive to the foundation of an ideal society.

Some of us climb trees more often than others. Very few of us have never climbed a tree at all, and it seems such a natural thing for human beings to do (at any rate in youth) that it is strange to hear of a community where this innocent recreation is rigorously eschewed. PROFESSOR FRANK DEBENHAM records, in the current issue of the *Geographical Journal*, an encounter with this curious form of dendrophobia. He noticed that the aboriginal bushmen of the Kalahari Desert were unable to clamber without assistance on to the lorries of his expedition and at the end of their journey were equally incapable of jumping down from the vehicles without misjudging the distance and falling flat on their faces. When he asked them whether they never climbed, for the sake of a vantage-point while hunting, the low trees which abound in that region, they told him (in effect) not to be silly. The last thing they wanted to do was to see—and be seen by—their quarry at a distance ; all they were interested in was its tracks, which they are able to follow with uncanny skill. We never, they said firmly, climb trees.

The bushmen's attitude is entitled to respect, and as the nesting season gets under way many anxious nannies and governesses will wish that this attitude was included among the respects in which a resemblance could be traced between their little charges and these remote and backward savages. In the ordinary citizen it will instil a measure of increased self-confidence, a feeling that, over-civilized though he is, he yet has an unexpected superiority over the unspoiled children of nature. His diet may not be all that much better than theirs, which has a basis of " roots, tubers, and such small fry as mice and frogs " ; and if given a bow and some poisoned arrows and shown a week-old spoor it might be some time before giraffe appeared upon his menu. But at least he can climb up the easier sort of tree and, apparently as a consequence of this, he does not measure his length in the highway every time he descends from a bus.

THE SOOTHING SIX-SHOOTER

An international conference on youth education, held under the auspices of Unesco and attended by 600 experts, has been told that cowboy films are a Good Thing. It was actually put (by the professor of criminology at Luxembourg University) more precisely than that; these films, he said, " have an actual psycho-therapeutic effect on the mind." The epithet, as every schoolboy knows, means " of or pertaining to the treatment of mental or psychic disease," but from other remarks attributed to the professor it does not appear that he considers the beneficent influence of Westerns to be restricted to youths who are already maladjusted or mentally deranged. They are a tonic which does you good even if you do not particularly need it.

Hitherto, in this country at any rate, the cowboy has been regarded as a mildly subversive influence. In the very young he has been suspected of, on the one hand, causing nightmares and, on the other, of encouraging the promiscuous discharge of cap-pistols—a side-arm curiously and rather unfortunately resembling his own six-shooter in its ability to go on firing almost indefinitely without having to be reloaded. It is almost certainly true that, were it not for cowboy films, far more little girls would blossom into gracious womanhood without having suffered, in the early stages of that process, the humiliation of being lassoed with the nursery clothes-line; and the horsier type of family may be pardoned for regarding the cowboy, with his penchant for galloping down precipitous slopes and his habit of pulling his pony back on to its haunches in order to stop it, as a dangerous influence.

Now that we know he is psycho-therapeutic, we can breathe again. We never, of course, doubted that his ends were chivalrous ; it was only that we sometimes wondered whether they justified his means. He managed to do, in one way or another, an enormous number of things that we had been careful to impress on our children were never done by nice people. Though not often indoors, he always kept his hat on when he was. He seldom knocked before entering a room, being far more likely to put a bullet through the lock and then kick the door open. He did not wear a tie, or clean his teeth before lying down in his poncho under a full moon. He omitted to say his prayers and he never cleaned his gun, which he frequently and deliberately pointed at people. Though admirably courteous to the opposite sex, he was all too successful in concealing any scruples he may have felt when engaged, as he so often was, in shooting Red Indians ; and though ostensibly and at times mawkishly fond of his horse he broke almost all the rules connected with its management, invariably bringing it home at a gallop and making dreadfully unacceptable use of his bit, his spurs, and his quirt. No one will wish to question the verdict pronounced in his favour by a professor of criminology ; but it might have carried more weight—in the Shires, at any rate—if it had been endorsed by a professor of veterinary science.

GUILTY SPLENDOUR

The expression " an officer and a gentleman " is now not very often heard. It has come to sound undemocratic and pretentious. To progressive thinkers commissioned rank is *per se* an institution of questionable value, and many would be happier if in HER MAJESTY's forces the responsibilities of command could be discharged by some process which did not involve the creation of what they are apt to call an " officer class." This stronghold of privilege and reaction has been, in its time, the target for some pretty harsh criticism, but it can seldom have been subjected to a more searching and ruthless analysis than it was the other day by a Russian periodical called *Odesskiye Novosti.*

The British officer, says this fearless magazine, is spoilt, capricious, and *blasé*. It is difficult to see how he could be anything else, for " his income runs into several thousands, often tens of thousands, a year, of which he keeps no account, being incapable of keeping accounts." His conditions of service, though unsatisfactory in some respects (" the pay he receives from the Government hardly suffices to keep him in perfume and gloves "), are in others enviable. " English officers, especially young ones, do absolutely no work of any kind. They spend their days and nights in clubs of extraordinary magnificence and opulence." It is not surprising that the average officer's morals leave something to be desired; " he is usually occupied with two girl friends simultaneously, a lady of high society and a girl from the ballet or opera." English uniforms, the article notes, are " truly magnificent, and cut to fit very tight," and it is largely for the sake of wearing them that the British officer enters the service. In the circumstances we cannot wonder that this slothful though aromatic popinjay is " the most ignorant officer in Europe from a professional point of view."

The cogency of these criticisms is enhanced by two factors. The first is that, though they are made by a foreign observer, they echo (though it must be admitted that they also tend to amplify) complaints against the British officer which are often voiced in thoughtful sections of the community to whose defence he is supposed to be dedicated. The second and more important factor is their patent objectivity. However ready MARSHAL STALIN may be to admit the comparative improbability of an immediate conflict, no conceivable interest of Russian policy or propaganda can be served by proving, in terms so incontrovertible, that one of the principal armies theoretically poised for agression against the U.S.S.R. is virtually incapable of coming under starter's orders. You cannot double the parts of Hotspur and Roderigo. If all the officers of the British Army are useless, some at least of their opposite numbers in the Red Army must be redundant ; and one would like to think that *Odesskiye Novosti* has lit a torch which, when it has been handed on through the proper channels, may lead to a certain number of people in either camp sloughing off their tight, but truly magnificent, uniforms.

THE EVENT OF THE EVENING

Peering back into the mists of history, we may conjecture that the practice of making after-dinner speeches owed its origin to administrative convenience. Only at meal times did the centripetal counteract the centrifugal tendencies of tribal life in Ancient Britain ; in other words, after dinner was the time to say anything if you wanted everyone to hear it. At what stage this sensible custom began—fatally—to enlarge or to diverge from its original purpose it is impossible to say. Somebody, perhaps, dropped in accidentally from a neighbouring cave and, by some misinterpretation of the laws of hospitality, was prevailed on to say a few words after the chief had finished making his announcement about the need for economy in the use of the new swept-back arrowheads. The stranger, having nothing practical to say and knowing little about his hosts, burbled on, told the latest shaggy mammoth story, and sat down amid applause. Thus (it seems highly probable) came vestigially into being the after-dinner speech as we know it, to our cost, to-day.

It still, of course, survives in its very earliest form. Presidents—briefed by the treasurer—usefully address those over whom they preside. Facts and figures which are, or should be, of interest to the diners are set forth, often at considerable length. Of this (as it may be termed) tribal form of after-dinner speech there can be few criticisms in principle ; it is a necessary evil. But the now widespread practice of bringing in someone from outside the tribe to display his virtuosity as an orator has little to commend it. To persons of refinement there is something peculiarly sickening about the painstaking but flimsy pretence that the tribe know all about the stranger and the stranger is deeply interested in the tribe. " There is no need for me," says the chief, glancing sideways and downwards at the hunched, hopeless figure beside him, " to introduce Mr. Slingsby Pott-Boyle to members of our society. We have all of us read his books." (Here the stranger observes several people to crane forward and stare at him in astonishment and a deaf ex-president two places away is heard muttering hoarsely, " Didn't know the feller wrote. Did you ? ") " You will not need to be reminded," the chief continues, putting on his spectacles so as to be able to misread a short dossier compiled by the secretary from a standard work of reference, " you will not need to be reminded that our guest, in addition to his literary activities, had a fine record in the last war, when he served in the—er—" (here the chief fails to decipher the secretary's handwriting) "—in one of—er—the finest regiments in the Army and—er—became a major."

By this time the night is apt to be far advanced. What with a long statement by the treasurer and a series of incomprehensible personal allusions from a retiring vice-president which set the table repeatedly in a roar, the evening's programme is behind schedule; and when the speaker rises to his feet, a fair number of the audience rise to theirs too and leave the room precipitately. It is now up to the stranger to pretend familiarity with and long-standing respect for the tribe, about whom he knows nothing and cares less. " Indeed an honour . . . society with a record like yours . . . maintaining this fine tradition. . . . Not for me to try to improve on your president's definition of . . . ." He staggers through this insincere preamble, then launches out of the tribal shallows into the fishy and forbidding depths of after-dinner humour. If his speech is a success, his audience do not spare a thought for the painful ordeal which preceded its delivery; if it is a failure, he for his part is equally callous to the sufferings he inflicts on them. It is rarely that all concerned do not come away chastened by the experience they have shared; and it seems all the more remarkable that next time the tribe have a dinner they will once again arrange for a stranger to deliver an after-dinner speech, which they all unite in hoping will be better than last time. It seldom is.

EAVESDROPPING IN ABSENTIA

The pleasure which we derive from the use of the telephone varies in its intensity according to our natures. Some of us abominate the invention, employing it only with the utmost reluctance and speaking into it in tones which convey our disapproval of the whole procedure. To others it seems a heaven-sent medium of communication, obviating virtually all necessity to write letters and greatly enlarging the daily scope for polite conversation. Between these two extremes are graded lesser degrees of abhorrence or enthusiasm, the golden mean being probably represented by those who regard the telephone system as a form of social plumbing without which, though it is sometimes tiresome and always expensive, life would be rather more difficult than it is already.

Of the various experiences which are, or may be, incidental to the making of a telephone call one of the most fascinating is not touched on in the literature on the subject issued to subscribers by the Postmaster-General. When the caller gets the right number but the wrong person he is sometimes given valuable though tantalizing opportunities for eavesdropping. " Hullo ! " says a childish voice, very loudly. " Is Mrs. Smith in ? " inquires the caller. " Yes. Why ? " The caller intimates that he would like to speak to Mrs. Smith. " He says," announces the childish voice, which although still deafeningly loud is apparently directed to a third party, " he wants to speak to Mummy." " Ask him who he is, silly," directs the third party. " O.K.," says the spokesman of the Smith family. " Who are you ? " The caller says that he is Mr. Jones, a piece of intelligence instantly retransmitted to the third party. The third party is sceptical. " It can't be Mr. Jones," she points out. " He's dead." The caller, intervening, affirms that he is another Mr. Jones and could they please ask their Mummy to come to the telephone. There is a crash as the receiver is dropped, and the receding sound of a stampede, and distant, disembodied voices can be heard acquainting their mother of the fact that she is wanted on the telephone by—extraordinary coincidence—a person called Mr. Jones who is nevertheless not the same as the Mr. Jones who worked in the dairy and died and went to heaven.

Sometimes the (as it were) sound pictures we get of the reception of our telephone calls have unflattering implications. " Tell him I'm out." " I can't, dear. I said you were in." " Oh, all right then. But I wish you'd have a little more gumption." Whispered colloquies such as these are not the happiest prologue to a telephone conversation. On the whole, though, we gain more than we lose by listening at long range to sounds in other people's houses that we were never meant to hear. Who would have thought that Robinson sang in his bath? And that angry exclamation—" Get out of my way, curse you ! "—which Harris uttered as he approached the instrument—was that addressed to Mrs. Harris or to her almost equally unsympathetic Pekinese? Telephoning has got much more interesting since the days when even the largest house boasted only one instrument, and, once the butler's ponderous footsteps had died away across the parquet, there was nothing—not even their wireless—to listen to as one waited and waited and waited

LEONARDO'S LEFT HAND

Doubts were recently thrown by a correspondent in these columns on the left-handedness of LEONARDO DA VINCI. That he used his left hand predominantly was admitted, but he was denied the full status of a "right cerebral-hemisphere-dominant individual." These, for some laymen at least, are dark and intriguing words, and their author, MR. NORMAN CAPENER, has now expanded his argument in an article published in the *Lancet*. He examines the evidence that LEONARDO's earliest notes were written mirror fashion and that his right hand may have been crippled in an accident. LEONARDO is quoted as remarking that he "thanked God for having escaped from murderers with only one hand dislocated." The conclusion is reached that, for the more dynamic drawing of shape and structure, LEONARDO probably used his right hand, but, for the contemplative aspects of shading and writing, he used his left.

If this is so, he shared a confusing measure of ambidexterity with many sportsmen and women. It is not impossible to find girls who bat—and knock their brothers for six—left-handed, but play hockey and lacrosse the other way round. Cricketers, including some of the most famous, display a da Vincian versatility. An eleven could be picked of players, headed by FRANK WOOLLEY and JAMES LANGRIDGE, who bat and bowl left-handed. Against it an opposing side of half-and-halfers would show RHODES, F. R. FOSTER, COMPTON, and VERITY batting right and bowling left, and CLOSE and M. S. NICHOLS bowling right and batting left. The game would be watched by serried ranks of elderly rabbits, who blame their feeble performances at the wicket on the foolish insistence of authority in their childhood on the correction of their natural left-handed stonce. Salt is rubbed into the wounds of these sufferers from old-fashioned and outmoded prejudice against left-handedness by the sympathy shown, nowadays, to what may be called the sinister way of taking a grip of things.

From being frowned upon, the left-handers have turned militant. The Society of Left Handed Golfers, which claims that there are some three hundred such players belonging to clubs in London and the Home Counties, is holding, next month, an open amateur competition from which mere right-handers are properly excluded. A sister society in America publishes a journal in which an old baseball player asks, somewhat apprehensively, whether he is fit to associate with fully qualified " lefties." His dilemma is that, while he batted left-handed and hits all his woods and irons that way, he lapses, when putting, to the right. A defensive League of Strong Right-handers may soon be needed. Its members can appeal to the psychologists of Chicago who found that left-handedness in rats is due to an absence of Vitamin B and that these intelligent animals, when deserting a sinking ship, vault the bulwarks in the right-paw style. Appeals of this sort are liable to come back as boomerangs and it will be safer to stick to old masters on the subject. Dismissing STEELE, who described some left-handed experts at single rapier, the last word can be left—by the right-handers—to Don Quixote. " For thou must know, O Sancho ! " he said, " that, for a man to be left-handed, argues that neither good example nor good teaching could reach him." Unfortunately, Don Quixote is not everybody's ideal of the convincing witness.

EPPUR SI MUOVE

The time is coming at jet speed when it will be quicker to go round the world than round the town. Our AERONAUTICAL CORRESPONDENT, who breakfasted and dined in London yesterday, lunched in Rome. Had he taken a train to Birmingham or Bristol, the journey would have lasted as long as did his Comet flight. Had he caught a bus in the City, bound for the West End, he might have passed Temple Bar about as soon as, in fact, he crossed the Channel. The virtues of this " cannon ball service," as SIR MILES THOMAS calls it with justifiable pride, are obvious. Taking up the telephone, on which he has failed to get a toll call to his home in Surrey, the future captain of industry will be put through in a twinkling to Singapore. A few well chosen words, explaining that he cannot start to-night until after dinner, and he will be expected for supper to-morrow in the Malay States. Such progress will surely save him from any nostalgic regrets for the past in which he could reach his club as fast on wheels as on foot.

Sober sense will tell him that, as a globe trotter, he is the luckiest heir of all the ages, but, even so, he may be betrayed into a sigh of envy of his fathers who were globe potterers. They escaped from their desks to enjoy carefree days or weeks dozing in comfortable cabins, picking their way between the deck tennis players and rubbing up their bridge through long, leisurely tropical evenings in the smoking saloon. When they reached their journey's end, they strode ashore, healthy as sandboys, to astonish their business contacts with displays of masterful negotiation. An air trip, however luxurious, denies the tired fellows this breather. Some of them will say that they were always bored by ships and that they descend, after hours in flight, fresh and fit as fiddles. Others confess to experiencing a hangover, that may be delayed for a day or two, brought on by novel experience and hectic change of place. A few candid voyagers have confessed that, on some of their lightning visits, they only came well and truly to the surface on getting back to the office desks they had so lately deserted.

Progress in the amenities as well as in the pace of air travel is rapidly removing some of the old inconveniences. When sea and rail first began to be challenged—and for years afterwards—aircraft had much in common with stage coaches. They started at unearthly hours, involved brief and unsettling stops by the way, and often gave those who patronized them a jolting to be remembered. Their windows offered glimpses of the landscape as tantalizingly incomplete as must have been enjoyed from an inside seat in a coach. Anyone who had flown in a smaller and more open machine was bored in a passenger airliner. Now that so many of these limitations to wholehearted rejoicing in progress are disappearing and the rest will, no doubt, follow them into history, they should not be forgotten. The first age of everyday long-distance flying is coming to an end and it deserves to be kept on the record of the social chronicle. The Comet is blazing a new trail that will make its predecessors seem as old-world as a clipper. Sitting pensively in his crawling bus, the stay-at-home may reflect, with what philosophy is at his command, that, in the past, he could not afford the time and, now, he cannot afford the money to go places in a big, bold, global way.

C. B. FRY

If MR. CHARLES BURGESS FRY had never been born, as, fortunately, he was, eighty years ago to-day and in Surrey of all Home Counties, it would have been necessary to invent him. The authors of serial stories in a boy's own paper—say in *C. B. Fry's Magazine*—had to learn that life is not a bed of roses. They, feebly letting truth set the pace for fiction, had for long allowed their heroes a blue or two, a goal here, a try there, a decent show in school sports, and just enough book-learning to avoid rustication. More than that, they feared, was over the odds of probability, and then a Reptonian was elected Senior Scholar of Wadham, with the future Lord Birkenhead coming in fourth. After that, fiction gave up the race and sat gasping in amazement while truth sprinted off down the straight. The facts about MR. FRY's record as an undergraduate are so famous and so familiar that any writer must blush to recite them in detail. Captain of Oxford against Cambridge at cricket and at Association football was not enough—a century had to be made at Lord's (not out, of course), and a blue for Rugby football only missed through a last-minute accident. A performance for the O.U.D.S. as the Prince of Morocco in *The Merchant of Venice* crowded a second night house to enjoy an athletic rendering of the line "Oh, Hell, what have we here ?" A meeting with MR. MAX BEERBOHM of Merton led to the coining of the phrase "Golf is glorified croquet." A taste for taking exercise against Cambridge, without the distractions of a ball, caused the setting up of a world's record for the long jump.

Those were salad days' triumphs. The best was yet to come. Among the many good reasons for having been alive and taking notice in the earliest years of this century must have been that K. S. RANJITSINHJI and C. B. FRY were Sussex batsmen together. This partnership, it has been said, turned MR. FRY from a good to a great player. He needed little turning. Upright at the wicket, with bat lifted back over the middle stump, he made the Hove ground seem too small to contain a cricket-ball. His straight drives and his on strokes were a delight and, when deluded fielders suspected him of being weaker to the off, he taught them better. Statistics embalm the thousands of runs in a season and the row upon row of centuries. They cannot recapture the grace of the artist at the wicket. The saddest might-have-been of the game is that this perfection of batsmanship was never seen in Australia.

Sport, even at this high Olympian level, had to take its place in the queue of MR. FRY'S accomplishments. He has written well in prose and verse. He has stood as a Liberal for Parliament. His long service in the Mercury rightly earned him at the age of seventy-four the honorary rank of Captain, R.N.R. A horseman and an angler, a marksman and a motorist, he has preserved through all his strenuous versatility as an out-of-doors man an unquenchable zest for good talk. Those who have been privileged to hear him agree that there is no subject, from Greek music to the gold standard, in which he will drop a catch. The great sportsman is a good companion and his memories are rich. He recalls MEREDITH asking him if the whip stroke was better than the long swing, and BARRIE—that ardent amateur of cricket—" not minding a bit " when his Scottish terrier nipped her fellow-countryman in the Achilles tendon. With so much gaiety and such well-earned fame behind him, MR. FRY should go forward confidently to complete his century.

OLE MAN ENGLISH

An American visitor, having kept his ear closely to the ground in Yorkshire, Wales, and London, has just come to the refreshing conclusion that pure English is spoken only in Alabama. This is a challenge to the Scots and Irish, who have, hitherto, so largely had the field to themselves in laying down the law on how English should be pronounced. They disagree among themselves on almost all points of detail, except that Cockney is a miserable, nasal symptom of cold in the head and that an Oxford accent is worse. These basic principles being accepted as axiomatic, the debate has gone on merrily over the years, with only here and there an English voice getting a hearing. When it has ventured to speak above a whisper, more often than not the bold exception comes from the north country. A gallant but forlorn claim was made some time ago for Somerset, but this was laughed out of court by critics of the west country who argued that the standard for English must not be " Ef so be 's 'ee want to go to Zisseter, why don't 'ee zay zo ? " Order was only restored by a general onslaught on poor old south-eastern English which was accused of being uncertain as to whether ass should rhyme with grass or with lass. The standards of the south were dismissed as no better than shadowy relics of the more racy and coloured talk of our ancestors.

Now the Celtic and northern pundits face attack from an unprotected flank, and they no longer have SHAW to lead them into battle. It is even doubtful whether the B.B.C., which in the past has so often rushed in where Englishmen fear to tread, will be ready for another war. Wounds at Broadcasting House still smart. That doughty old warrior " Conduit," for all the broadcast fire directed against him, has not yet abandoned the two syllables in which he dug himself into his street. Conduit continues defiantly to come off some tongues in rhyme with pundit and not, roughly, with cruet. Accent stays put, in spite of opposition from the microphone, on the first syllable of disputant. Half-hearted confessions, ominous for the morale of the once confident invaders of the south, have been made. A Lancashire man has admitted that, after trailing the clouds of his native speech into the unconsonanted and vowelly south, he has become, like other migrants, an irredeemable mongrel.

This new American threat does hold out some hope at least for Yorkshire. The Alabama challenger admits that, in local idiosyncrasy, Yorkshiremen remain unbeatable. They change their dialect, so he says, every ten miles. That is what they themselves have long said. At their most militant stage, they declared that any student of phonetics knows that the dialect of Pogmoor is not that of Old Town, Barnsley, half a mile away. Pilley differs, they assert, from Elsecar and Cawthorne from Huddersfield. An old cutlery dialect is reputed to have survived in Sheffield and the speech of Doncaster to resemble that of the capital more than that of Goole on the one hand or of Wakefield on the other. Teaming up with their neighbours towards the Scottish border, they have claimed that the dialect spoken in Cleveland and just south of the Esk is the best surviving representative of the ancient language of Northumbria. Dialect is better than nothing and these claims should be consolidated if the palm for purity has gone to Alabama. Whether it has may be left for Boston (Mass) to settle. Boston (Lincs) and the rest of us, digesting the case made out for the Deep Southerner, may recall what JOWETT said of one of the exploits of ELIJAH: "Perhaps he did."

VANITY FAIR

It may be more than a coincidence that the most celebrated of English Victorian caricaturists, PELLEGRINI, was an Italian born in Capua and that the greatest living master of this mocking art has been too long in exile at Rapallo. What a German critic once called " the sour bilious temper of John Bull " has rarely in recent times expressed itself in drawing. Judged by the general run of caricatures, John Bull is a good-natured chap, given amiably to showing his leaders as animals or birds, and seldom, after he has grown up and ceased to libel the form master in the fly leaves of school books, letting himself go with much real bite. Here and there there is an exception and, as the retrospective exhibition which has just opened in London brings out, SIR MAX BEERBOHM is one of them. MR. DAVID LOW, who has just brought out a new volume of caricatures, is another. Both these artists, who strike deep but are seldom cruel, look back nostalgically to the past. SIR MAX BEERBOHM notes that, about twenty years ago, he realized that he was no longer seeing people in terms of caricature, but was making pleasant likenesses of them and had better lay aside his pencil. MR. LOW regrets that contemporary fashion lends itself less and less to expression of personality.

It is uncertain what reception hard-hitting caricature would receive to-day. The knock-about, prize-fighting technique, which once went down well in Britain and is still popular in Europe and in America might startle a generation given so readily to awarding damages to aggrieved parties and to solemn protests by offended members of Parliament. That musicians have lately been arguing in favour of doing their own criticism and dispensing with critics is a small sign of the times. Tolerant readiness to assume that the pianist is doing his best and not to shoot him runs through many walks of life. Yet satire, which has grown on the whole so gentle and so good-mannered and so lacking in punch in drawing, has kept up more vigorously in print. SWIFT himself was not more savage than ORWELL and the past might be raked in vain for satire more deeply mordant than that of the early MR. EVELYN WAUGH. The age may, after all, be ready to face self-criticism such as individual Edwardians from the KING downwards had to take from SIR MAX BEERBOHM. There is a wealth of material to hand. Vanity Fair no longer has peers or plutocrats, smugly comfortable middle-class magnates, or overbearing society ladies to serve as targets. New types are dominant, but they are no less candidates for deflation. The revolution of the last ten years has caused so drastic a general post that the caricaturist may be excused for being bewildered in his aim, but there is no lack of fair game.

THE VILLAGE GREEN

What a sunset is to the amateur in water-colours, what robins and coach-and-four careering through a snowy countryside, with jolly gentlemen waving from the box, are to designers of Christmas cards, so, at this season of the year, is the village green to those who delight in composing themes on the subject of the old and honourable contest between bat and ball. It matters not at all that the pitfalls are as deep as they are obvious, that the saga of the blacksmith, his trousers kept up by a complex alliance between braces and string, hitting the vicar for six and winning the needle match of the season has been sung by a thousand voices, that the description of the clock of the village church chiming out the tranquil evening hours as the players go through the ritual of their game is apt to degenerate into a facile sentimentality, and that there is nothing, positively nothing, new that can be said about the annual contest between Much Binding and Lesser Lightfold. The mind reaches, nevertheless, for phrases on rustic peace, the spirit of the countryside and the symbolism of cricket in its relation to life. Quotations from Miss Mitford to de Selincourt pick themselves, and the heart and the meaning of England are found in the meeting of two cricket teams on a square of grass out in the middle of a meadow.

The trouble is that the sternest realist, going out with the resolute intention of debunking village cricket and all that it stands for, is apt to find that Nature is up to her old trick of imitating art and that the village cricket match of essay, poem, and fiction is disconcertingly like the village cricket match of fact. To be sure, there are differences of detail and emphasis. Blacksmiths, with or without braces, are in short supply, and the proportion of white in the clothing colour scheme of white, black, grey, and blue is steadily rising; but the spirit and form of the thing obstinately refuse to be exorcized. "The lads from the forge and the barn and the mill and the fold," and others who are not lads, continue to hit cheerfully across the flight of the ball and to find an immense pleasure in doing so, and even the occasional quarrels and upsets, the local feuds and jealousies, serve only to throw into brighter relief the general atmosphere of good fellowship. The man who sets out to decry or ignore the village green will, if he is wise, know that he is beaten. The game is already on and the status of the cow, as Mr. Robertson-Glasgow puts it, has changed from that of tenant to spectator.

THE GAY GARDENERS

Strange sights are seen in the King's Road round the seasons, but none so strange or more welcome to Chelsea as the annual visitation of gardeners. Thick as roses on a bush in June, thick almost as the greenfly on the same bush, the initiates of the cult amiably lose their way as they potter along the town streets, dreaming of triumphs to come in the home village show. Dr. Watson himself, had he been a Chelsea man of any standing, would have been able to tell one of these annual migrants at a glance. Stray specimens pass through at other times of the year, but the student-watcher does not bother about them, preferring to wait and see them in one fell swoop in May. Some connoisseurs maintain that the spectacle is at its finest on the day of the private view, but others prefer the day when first the horticultural floodgates are opened. Fullest delight in this annual display can only be taken by a member of that unfortunate minority in British society which goes through life without learning to tell one flower from another. Anyone else, however slight his knowledge and interest, is liable to be sucked into the treacherous currents of enthusiasm that are now flowing to and from the Embankment.

Why is it that these gardeners stand out so remarkably in a London crowd? They are of all ages. They are drawn from what, once upon a time, were called different social classes. They wear no labels, and yet they would not be more clearly labelled if they sported huge green rosettes and waved rattles in the manner of a cup tie invasion. What betrays them is that they all look so outrageously happy. Theirs is a fanaticism that seems to inoculate them, at any rate on these occasions of

K—2

high festival, against the cares of the contemporary world. It may be that they are gaily conscious that they are breaking all the rules—or most of them—of the age of the common man. They form a blatant aristocracy; indeed, while one is about it, one may as well tell the whole truth and call them a plutocracy. They glory in their wealth. What, by competitive wrestling, they win from their flower beds and vegetable plots they flaunt (politely but none the less flaunt) in the faces of less lucky rivals.

A man with the mark of gardening upon him ceases to take count of the number of hours he works. He even ceases to mind being described as highbrow—an epithet that in any other context would fill him with shame and rage. Specialists in all other branches of knowledge except gardening have to go slow in Britain and to apologize for using difficult words and pretend that they regard themselves as just ordinary chaps. There is none of that democratic nonsense about gardeners. Their memory for difficult names is astonishing to the uninstructed and they make no disguise of their astonishment at his lack of instruction. English and Latin are all the same to them and, as may be tested by eavesdropping these days in any Chelsea teashop, they can go on indefinitely and blissfully talking to one another in a language that is Greek to the outsider. Frustration, depression, fear, envy, and every complex known to the psychiatrists flee before the gaiety of the gardeners. Almost they persuade a heathen to start a window-box.

A CARAVAN OF BATS

Neither the Foreign Office nor the M.C.C. has seen fit to comment on a report from Kalimpong that a large consignment of cricket bats, transported on the backs of mules, is on its way to Lhasa at the behest of the education authorities in Tibet. Accustomed as we are to being baffled by international affairs, it is difficult to recall any recent development in that sphere of which the significance was harder to evaluate. There is, of course, nothing odd in the Tibetans wanting to play cricket; this natural and salutary aspiration does them credit. The mountain torrents of their native land and her frequently frozen lakes severely limit the opportunities open to wet-bobs, and it was perhaps inevitable that a passion for our national sport, repressed for centuries, should break out sooner or later.

It is, all the same, a little surprising that King Willow should come into his own at a time when Tibet is under Communist control. It may, of course, be that the new régime in Lhasa sees in cricket an opiate or anodyne which will confer upon the people partial oblivion of their sufferings; and it is certainly true that the history of the game is unsullied by any connexion with counter-revolutionary activity. But there are, after all, other sports less closely associated with the Imperialist tradition; and, however much one reveres cricket and however little one knows about Tibet, it is difficult to believe that this incomparable game is ideally suited to the conditions obtaining on the Roof of the World.

There may—indeed there must—be more in this business than meets the eye. It looks like some sort of a move in the Cold War. Readers with romantic minds will toy with the idea that the whole thing has been organized, for subversive purposes, by the British Secret Service—that at the head of the caravan (humming the Eton boating song to put people off the scent) strides, heavily disguised, some agent of the calibre of Colonel Egham or Big White Carstairs. Alas, it is more likely to be the other way round. World Communism, though it has many conquests to its credit, has as yet made little impression on cricket; but its outward indifference to the sport (the Russians have not even bothered to claim that they invented it) may well mask a respect for its civilizing influence and a determination to adapt it to conform with the exigencies of Marxist doctrine. It is true that Tibet does not seem a particularly sensible place in which to initiate this project; but it is remote and secluded, and the inhabitants have no preconceived bourgeois ideas on the subject which need to be eradicated. It seems all too probable that the report from Kalimpong may foreshadow the launching of a vast conspiracy throughout the New Democracies to undermine the influence of cricket by evolving a similar but ideologically sounder game. How fast or how far this threat to one of our dearest institutions may develop it is impossible to say. It depends, to a certain extent, on whether the people in Lhasa remembered to order any balls.

FREEDOM TO SKIP

There may not be many advantages in being grown-up, but there is at any rate one; the ARCHBISHOP of YORK will not insist on our finishing a book, once we have begun it, whether we like it or not. This, he says, is now and then very good discipline for a boy, but we who are older need not continue the unequal struggle. There are various motives that can impel us to go on ploughing through a book long after we are bored. There is first of all what THOMAS HUGHES called " the consciousness of silent endurance so dear to the heart of every Englishman," a quality which, in spite of his unquestioned greatness, he could sometimes himself evoke. Then there is the knowledge that the book is a classic and that it is the part of an educated man to have at least forgotten it. Memory recalls one, of a wide and admirable taste in literature, who observed " I only finished *Joseph Andrews* by repeated charges at the point of the bayonet." There is the desire, mild but insistent, to know what happens and who marries whom, or in the case of thrillers, and DR. GARBETT expressly admits an occasional thriller, who did it. Two rather more particular reasons are that somebody has given us the book or the author is a friend of ours, so that in either case we must be prepared to withstand cross-examination.

To be made to read a book is some way towards loathing it. During Mr. Wooster's brief engagement to Lady Florence Craye she made him read a book called *Types of Ethical Theory*, of which he remarked bitterly that it was doubtless all true but " not the sort of thing to spring on a lad with a morning head." Apart from so extreme a case, there are at least two dangers in the suggested compulsion. One is that it may implant a lasting hatred in the young gentleman's breast for a book which, had he begun it a year or so later, would have been his friend for life. The other, applicable both to boys and grown-ups, is that under any such hypothetical law nothing but short stories would be read and so, ultimately, written. The mere mass of pages would appal all but the bravest who would venture on *War and Peace*, and what a passion of pleasure many people would have lost by their cowardice! As to SIR WALTER SCOTT, one glance at the first chapter would too often be enough. What is needed by one beginning, for example, *Ivanhoe*, is that a kindly Archbishop should take the young reader by the hand and bid him never mind the Normans and Saxons, but start with Gurth and Wamba and "The Curse of St. Withold upon these infernal porkers!" Among all the freedoms which are to-day so peculiarly precious we must never forget the freedom to skip.

IN THE THICK OF IT

No praise is too high for the man in the street, as he used to be called as though he had no home to go to, or the "common" man, as he is now fashionably, if unflatteringly, described. When history is being made he is always there, playing a manful part and getting, it is true, credit for it as a type. As an individual he is too seldom remembered and the rare occasions of his recognition deserve to be noted. GENERAL WEYGAND has just provided one in his recently translated war memoirs. He is telling how, at the height of the horrors and confusion of the German break-through in 1940, he, the newly appointed French commander, landed on a forward airfield. He expected to be met there by senior officers who would conduct him to the KING of the BELGIANS and to the British commander, LORD GORT. Drama in a big way was afoot, but the principal actors were missing. Nobody could be found on the airfield until at last, the General records, he and his party met "a small soldier, very dirty, but with an attractive face." Thus, suddenly, does the common man cease to be a type and turn into a real live person. The limelight for once was played on a worthy, devoted, generally neglected and, we may be sure, infinitely embarrassed head.

This small soldier, wishing, perhaps, that he were not so very dirty, and unaware—it is pretty safe to guess—that his face seemed attractive to the General, told what he knew of the situation. It could not have been much, for his mind, as is the way of small soldiers, was on his own troubles. He asked what he was to do with 20,000 litres of petrol "about which he was greatly concerned, having received no orders." All the worst fears of all the old sweats from Marathon to Malaya and Korea are summed up in this encounter. Compared to it, the nightmare of walking down Bond Street naked at lunch time is an amusing dream. The anguish which the conscript candidate for immortality must have suffered scarcely bears thinking about. What, as he kept his lonely vigil, he must have been saying to himself, will happen if some scroungers get away with all this petrol, leaving no signatures behind them? Then, out of the blue, descends that aircraft and the hero of the day finds himself alone, face to face with the supreme brass hat. One likes to think that the small soldier, now snugly back in civvy street, often tells the tale over his *bock*. There is, we may be sure, an idiomatic French translation of "Cor blimey, you could have knocked me down with a feather," and, as that is heard in the estaminet, there is a sympathetic murmur of —Nom de something or other.

A bad quarter of an hour is worth the chance of remembrance for years to come. Other small soldiers, in and out of uniform, are lost in the crowd. The Greeks gave them a brief speaking part. When the tragic hero had inadvertently murdered his father or innocently eaten his children, baked like so many blackbirds in a pie, the little men of the chorus were issued with a ration of well-chosen words. "Ah, ah, this is a bad business" they would recite, "I much me fear that no good will come of it"—and they were faded out. BAIRNSFATHER saw them as Old Bill and STRUBE drew them in bowler hats. They were among those present at every sticky moment in the past, winning the battle, making the wheels of industry turn and paying the taxes. They are in the thick of it to-day and, being themselves, they will thank their lucky stars that they were not in the military boots of GENERAL WEYGAND'S small soldier.

THE GLOBE AT HARROW

Were it not for the irrelevant incursion of a flying bomb into Belmont on the Hill in 1944, the annual Harrow productions of SHAKESPEARE would now have attained a round dozen ; and since on that unfortunate occasion the *Merchant of Venice* had already been rehearsed, though the world never saw it, MR. RONALD WATKINS, the producer, may surely be allowed the benefit of the doubt. His has been a notable service to SHAKESPEARE, deserving of acknowledgment by a wider circle than the family of one school, however famous. This year, with *A Midsummer Night's Dream*, he maintains once more his conviction that the way to the full appreciation of the master's work is to reproduce the simple conditions of the Globe Theatre for which it was written. Practising in a kind of which the best are but shadows, he has dared to call upon the imagination of the audience to amend them, and they have been rewarded by finding that at every turn the poet's own words create for the mind's eye all that they require of a local habitation and a name.

Once the actors step out of the gilded frame of the eighteenth-century proscenium, and walk familiarly in the midst of the audience upon the Elizabethan platform that Harrow Speech Room can so easily reproduce, they can move from the palace of Duke Theseus to the enchanted wood without discomfort to the spectators, who could, if need be, accompany Puck as easily and put a girdle round about the earth in forty minutes. That is the theory, and it has been very largely proved in practice, as all who have seen the Harrow productions will testify. It does not of course follow that, because some obscured beauties are rediscovered by putting the picture back in its original frame, this way of producing Elizabethan drama is the only way. SHAKESPEARE himself, it may be surmised, would not necessarily have rejected, as an experienced actor, all the changes in theatrical architecture that other practical men devised after his time to overcome specific obstacles. Would he, for instance, have been quite so austere as MR. WATKINS, who denies himself even the darkening of the houselights in the closing scene of the benediction of the fairies, presumably because the poet had no electric-light switch to press? Nor, indeed, is the complete return to the Globe practicable; for the drama is an interplay between actors and spectators.

It is no longer possible to reproduce that essential element of the production of 1598, the minds, coloured by all the hues of a vanished century, that looked through Elizabethan eyes at, it may be, LORD SOUTHAMPTON'S wedding feast. So also, when at Bradfield next Saturday the eternal and unwritten laws are proclaimed again by Antigone from DR. GRAY'S exquisite miniature of the Athenian theatre, piety and scholarship cannot quite pour back into the words the precise sense they bore for men who heard them when PERICLES still presided over the city's destinies and the marble of the Parthenon gleamed white on the Acropolis. These attempts to recover the absolute meaning of a work of art by restoring the attendant circumstances of its creation still require a great imaginative effort to view them with the eyes of a vanished age. They represent, therefore, the student's approach to a masterpiece, which is no doubt the reason why they have best succeeded in schools; but there are some for whom that approach in itself diminishes enjoyment. The Harrow company might still retort that what they are really trying to recapture is the standpoint not of the audience at the Globe but of the Lord Chamberlain's Men who played there, and the conclusion of the argument may be that the highest and purest enjoyment of any art comes only to those who have tried, however humbly, to practise it, either as creators or as executants, for themselves.

COCKNEY KESTRELS

Film-stars, those not particularly rare migrants, are often reported to have " flown in " to London, and upon arrival in the metropolis they are occasionally prevailed upon to grant interviews in their hotel suites. The females are sometimes accompanied by their mates, whose plumage is less remarkable and who generally appear—anyhow in the photographs—to be rather smaller in size. It may well have been the precedent thus created which inspired a hen kestrel (as we reported yesterday) to fly into London and make her nest in the façade of a caravanserai much favoured by visitors from Hollywood. If she was after publicity she has got it; but it is permissible to wonder whether she is doing the right thing either by her husband or by the brood of fledglings which she and he are now nourishing on mice believed to be poached from the well stocked coverts on the Festival of Britain site.

There is, of course, a certain *réclame* attached to living in, or rather on, a luxury hotel, and although a mouse does not necessarily taste any better for having eaten holes in the underparts of the Dome of Discovery, it possibly acquires thereby some sort of *cachet.* But these, even to a hawk with social ambitions, are somewhat imponderable advantages. Against them must be set the drawbacks, from a kestrel's point of view, of living in a built-up area. Its chief and singular accomplishment is its ability to hover, poised statically in space with wing-tips quivering, its bright, fierce eyes scanning the floor of the miniature jungle far below it. But what is the point of hovering over (let us say) the Strand? You can get just as good a view by sitting prosaically among the sparrows on one of the splendid edifices with which this thoroughfare is lined. Nor, as you look downward, do you need a keener eyesight than the sparrow has. Even if the Strand were carpeted (which up to the time of going to press it was not) with lucerne or spring barley, confusingly rippled by the breeze, there are no field-mice to be discerned there. No doubt the kestrel, like the film-star, thinks that our policemen are wonderful; but even the finest constable, seen from above, does not present a spectacle calculated to appeal indefinitely to a hawk.

There are, of course, open spaces where the parents can swoop and glide and—one day—teach their young screamingly to fly, and in the latter process they will no doubt attract a gratifying amount of attention, but there will be a sad lack of variety about the creatures whom the hawks will see there. To himself, and to a less extent to passers-by, a Cabinet Minister striding across St. James's Park is an object of considerable interest, but he cannot mean very much to a kestrel, who would far rather get a glimpse of a vole. Looking ahead, moreover, to a day when the young are grown up and go out into a greener world to seek their fortune, may we not fear that they will find themselves, for all their sophistication, rather ill-equipped for life in the country? The silence will oppress them, and the darkness at night. Eyes which have grown bored invigilating over motor-buses and river steamers, Guardsmen in scarlet and an infinite variety of ladies' hats, may well be disconcerted by their first glimpse of a weasel, and the hawks may learn to their cost that there is a difference between the motionless figure of a stockbroker with a taste for bird-watching and the motionless figure of a gamekeeper with a gun. Still, they have made their decision, or rather their mother has made it for them, and while we may not all agree that it was a sound decision from the kestrels' point of view, Londoners will be glad of the chance of seeing (or saying that they thought they saw) these graceful hawks cutting across the cañons of the streets.

LISTENER-DRIVER

Peering into the future through his dust-blurred goggles, the inventor of the horseless carriage doubtless foresaw, in a rough and ready way, most of the main lines along which, as time went on, his invention would be improved. One day, he felt confident, automobiles would be constructed which would travel at speeds greater—perhaps much greater—than fifteen miles an hour. They would break down less frequently, they would be more commodious to travel in and their headlamps—thanks, probably, to the evolution of a weather-proof fusee—would be easier to light on stormy nights. They would make less noise and emit fewer fumes. They might be found to possess a limited, but none the less real, military value ; and there was no reason why, in the field of sport, races between automobiles might not become an attractive novelty. As the intrepid but unpopular fellow rattled along, he must have envisaged—in outline, at any rate—almost all the developments in the design and use of motor-cars that have in fact taken place. The one thing he did not, because he could not, foresee was that a day would come when the automobilist, by turning a knob, could listen as he drove along to disembodied voices singing dolefully about love, talking authoritatively about tree-frogs, or arguing petulantly about the welfare state.

Never (our mentors used to admonish us in early youth) try to do two things at once. It always seemed a rather pointless prohibition, regularly flouted by several of the people we most admired. Our parents, reading the newspaper while they ate toast and marmalade, were patently doing two things at once. It would have been ridiculous to pretend that the huntsman, blowing his horn as he cantered, lean and godlike, down the covertside, was only doing one thing at a time; and none of the conjurers we saw ever seemed to be doing less than about three. The listener-driver is certainly doing two things at once. Insulated already against the outside world by the container of glass and metal in which he bowls along, he is further protected against the tiresome realities of his journey by an incessant gush of soothing, stimulating, or edifying sound. He seems, on the whole, to like this arrangement.

Many listener-drivers, it may be presumed, are markedly regular in their habits. They drive between their home and their place of work at the same hour every day and become almost too familiar with the relevant phases of the B.B.C.'s programmes. Others, less bound by routine, find themselves plumbing unsuspected depths or (especially when a Test match is being broadcast) savouring unlooked-for delights. The general practitioner often gets a chance to note the striking resemblances between his own domestic life and that of the Dale family; and the farmer, returning from an implement sale, may steel himself to endure that *mauvais quart d'heure* during which, every evening, the realities of life in the country are presented by voices with the unmistakable burr of Kensington. The listener-driver disregards, with apparent impunity, the theory that nobody should be allowed to speak (let alone sing) to the man at the wheel, and he finds an agreeable distraction in listening to a great many things which he would not otherwise have heard. Sometimes, it is true, a programme proves boring; but in extreme cases—when, that is to say, the programme is even more boring than his own thoughts—he can always switch it off.

COIN OF THE REALM

Familiarity breeds inattention and few people (outside Scotland) could tell for certain, without first fishing into their pockets or handbags, on which coin to find Britannia and on which the ship. Coins remain, with stamps, the works of art most regularly seen. Their effigies and reverses are appealed to every day as heads and tails. From time to time, every one takes a close look at them and it is sometimes critical. To examine a random handful is to be reminded that the powers that be in this highly technical field have been less happy in the choice of some designs than of others. At one end of the scale of coins still in circulation is the charming "bun" penny, now alas so thin that it can almost be bent between the fingers. At the other and bottom end is that lamentable innovation of 1937, the clumsy twelve-sided threepenny bit—surely the least aesthetic little scrap of metal that ever found itself in the company of its betters in John Bull's purse.

A lovely young queen gives the opportunity for what DR. SUTHERLAND, in his presidential address to the Royal Numismatic Society, called last night "a most noble coinage." The committee set up, under the presidency of the DUKE of EDINBURGH, to advise the Royal Mint has a diverse and distinguished membership and it will, no doubt, take note of what DR. SUTHERLAND had to say on the need, in his view, to revise conditions and relax conventions. Sympathy will go out to the committee, for it has embarked on a most complex task. The gulf between the design of an artist on paper and what appears, after formidable technical processes, on a penny or a half-crown is almost as wide as that between an author and his work as it gets through on to a cinema screen.

Tradition and practical considerations add to the labours of this unfortunate committee and to the difficulties of the QUEEN herself. The final choice lies with her and she has to decide whether to follow the practice of changing the direction of the head. If she does so her profile will face to the right, as did that of her great-grandfather. This custom, which EDWARD VIII, for whom no coins were struck, had decided to break with, is traditionally traced back to the preference of CHARLES II for turning his back on CROMWELL.

The coins on which the new designs, fore and aft, are shown may themselves be varied. Enemies of the florin are again in the field and, no less militant, champions of a handy-sized five-shilling piece (to improve on the old cartwheel) and of a smaller penny. Even those perennially optimistic diehards, the advocates of the decimal system, have not given up all hope of weaning the British away from their loyalty to an arithmetic that brings frowns to the brows of foreign visitors. All in all, those responsible have their hands full. No one will wish to hurry them into rash decisions, especially when such forbidding precedents are recalled as the burst of ridicule that greeted one of the late Victorian effigies. They work in an age in which interest in good craftsmanship is keen and widespread and, if they can tell us how they are getting on, they can be sure of a friendly and critical audience.

A HUNDRED AND NINETY ASSES

A satirist, racking his brain for an original plot nowadays, must often feel tempted to despair. What really happens, particularly in the Alice in Wonderland world in which public bodies now seem to move, can give the creative imagination a big handicap and an easy beating. Suppose an undaunted satirist, determined to conquer new fields in fiction, evolved the following plot. Once upon a time, there were two public bodies. One had the custody, in a London goods depôt, of a hundred and ninety asses and the other accused the first of failing to provide adequate accommodation for those animals. Here the satirist would pause to ask himself in what conceivable circumstances could the bringing together of so many asses, in such a place, be made to appear probable to his readers. Encouraging himself with the faint hope that it will look alright in the proofs, he goes on to the next chapter. There the accused authority protests its innocence. The satirist thrusts aside the thought that, in real life, such a dispute would obviously be settled out of court. He needs a court scene and, throwing probability, as he fears, to the wind, he writes one.

In court the litigants appear—cheerful in the knowledge that all expenses will be paid by the public—and the action proceeds. The Diseases of Animals Act is invoked and the Transit of Horses Order. Under the Act, the expression " animal " is shown to include cattle, sheep, goats, and swine, but not horses and still less asses. The responsible Minister is accused of having failed to define horses as animals, as he might have done by taking advantage of a proviso that allows him to bring in any other kind of four-footed beast. Asses are, it is further shown, *de jure* horses, but, as neither has been given a legal look-in, it is too bad for both. The bench, entering into the Pickwickian spirit of the occasion, concurs, the defendants are awarded costs against their prosecutors, and every one is left completely in the dark as to what was in fact the fate of the allegedly ill-done-to asses.

At this point, if not before, the satirist begins to get cold feet and tries what he has written on his wife. She smiles a superior smile and tells him that he ought always to read the papers before beginning a day's work on fiction. His plot, more or less as he has sketched it, is just reported as having been played in real life by the Railway Executive and the London County Council. What is the poor satirist to do next? Probably he goes round to the two headquarters and asks to see MR. JOHN ELLIOT, chairman of the Railway Executive, and MR. EDWIN BAYLISS, chairman of the L.C.C. If he is lucky enough to find these busy citizens free for a chat, he asks them whether they are cutting in on his trade or whether, as he prefers to think, something may have gone wrong with the published reports of their little drama. He asks, too, about those hundred and ninety asses. What were they doing at the goods depôt and where are they now?

READING ROOM GHOSTS

To-day the Reading Room of the British Museum, elegantly redecorated, reopens to its votaries, exiled these eight months past. For some at least of them the place is haunted by nineteen ghosts—or by as many of them as any one reader can remember. They are the ghosts of those nineteen eminent writers of English (one must not say English writers, for SCOTT was among them) whose names, set out in large letters, from CHAUCER and CAXTON to TENNYSON and BROWNING in the spaces just below the windows of the dome, shed their message and influence upon the labouring scholar below. In those last years before 1914—secure because the basis of life, it seemed, could scarcely alter, exciting because so many enchanting new things were happening on its surface—the names around the dome were there to inspire and urge the reader to new efforts. SPENSER? Ah, yes, he must take down *The Faerie Queene* from the bedside shelf and really read it—read it, that is, without dozing off, the light extravagantly still burning, after about two-and-a-half delicious, somniferous stanzas. LOCKE? Well, the reader did not, admittedly, even own a copy of the *Human Understanding*, but undoubtedly he would do so, and read it too—one day. After 1914, or rather after 1918—for there was that unforgettable, unbridgeable, gap—it seemed, on the contrary, that the basis of almost anything might change, except perhaps the essential achievements of pure literature. And, for that almost despairingly cherished remnant of the unalterable values, those same names stood during the twenties and thirties—until in 1939 they were swept right away not by the flaming hailstones of war but by mere redecoration.

Few, in those years between the wars, doubted that the nineteen names were essential and original elements of the great dome, put there by PANIZZI himself; in fact they were, as symbols of the unchanging values, something of a humbug, dating from no longer than 1907, and selected, as it appeared upon inquiry, by so comparatively recent a pundit as SIR EDWARD MAUNDE THOMPSON. Then, the thought would come, what was the merit of this selection as a selection? CAXTON, TYNDALE, SHAKESPEARE, BACON—good—though CAXTON was more a printer than a literary man. MILTON and ADDISON—also good, but was there no place for DRYDEN between them? SWIFT, POPE, WORDSWORTH—yes, yes, but what about GRAY, and GOLDSMITH, and perhaps COWPER? GIBBON, of course—but great Heaven! where was JOHNSON? And why should BYRON have the preference over KEATS and SHELLEY? CARLYLE and MACAULAY, too, great guns as they were, could scarcely be allowed the victory over FIELDING, DICKENS, THACKERAY and, indeed, every novelist except SIR WALTER, and he (dreadful suspicion) might even have won his place as a poet.

In truth, there is material enough, and to spare, for two such lists of nineteen names; and it is easier to revise the old team by addition than by omission. BACON perhaps might go, and if the ardent Baconians complained, they could be reminded that, as they held him to be there already under a pseudonym, they could scarcely claim for him a second place, too. It is always tempting to play at this game of great names, and there will be many to wish that the present museum authorities—nay, let us be precise and say SIR THOMAS KENDRICK and MR. OLDMAN—had been willing to "have a go," even at the necessary cost of drawing invidious distinctions between the great men of old. When MAUNDE THOMPSON made his list, he may have felt doubts, but if so he brushed them aside, and stood by his choice. To-day we deal less in certainties, and put our own views forward, if at all, with diffidence. Perhaps that is what is wrong with us. We are not only unwilling to back our first eleven to win ; we are afraid even to give them their colours.

TAKE A LETTER

Every day, all over these islands, hundreds and thousands of men and women—some leaning back in their chairs with fingertips judiciously counterpoised, some standing in a kind of monolithic trance and gazing out of the office window, some pacing upon the managerial carpet like meditative carnivores—utter in mainly inexpressive voices a great, slow avalanche of words ; and every one of these words, as it drops from their lips, is transcribed, by a skilful subordinate using hieroglyphics, on to a pad and thence, with the help of a machine, on to a typescript. Considering both the extent to which communications within a modern society depend on dictation, and the prodigious number of man-hours devoted to it, it is surprising how little attention we pay to the technique of dictating. At school we were given only a rather specialized and exotic glimpse of this technique. " *Prenez,*" the French master used apprehensively to command, " *la dictée !* " After a short delaying action (" *S'il vous plaît, Monsieur, j'ai perdu la plume de ma tante* ") the class settled down to cope with the mysteries of *ouvrez les guillemets* and *point-virgule.* The dictator's enunciation was deliberate and limpid to the point of affectation ; but he was, after all, reading the stuff out from a book, and his methods gave us, in later life, little guidance in the crucial task of deciding what words, in what order, should best come after the invocation " Dear Sir."

To some people, no doubt, this task presents no difficulties. Orderly, succinct, well proportioned, their sentences come punctually on to parade, form themselves into paragraphs and march off under the streaming pennon of a three-decker reference number. These people are not seized periodically by a sort of coma or paralysis, during which everything to do with the matter in hand is expunged from their minds. They are not, during these bouts of wordlessness, tortured by remorse for the way in which they are wasting the valuable time of their secretary, nor covered with shame by the low estimate of their capacity as a man of affairs which she must be forming as she sits patiently but idly by. Nor do they, in order to end this humiliating *impasse*, suddenly dictate a sentence so jejune, so irrelevant, or so orotund that in the end the letter has to be retyped without it. Phrases like " Or have we said that already ? " and " I think perhaps you'd better leave that last bit out " do not constantly interrupt the even flow of their monologues. Nor do they ever experience the slightest difficulty in bringing a sentence to an end.

For those of us who will never attain their standards—the Er-men, the wafflers, the adders of explanatory postscripts in longhand—dictating a letter is rather like taking part in an obstacle race in thick fog. We are always getting entangled in conditional clauses, losing touch with our main verb and going back over the same ground. We can plead that it is not our fault—that, although we were trained in all other uses of the faculty of speech, from elocution to singing, nobody ever taught us how to dictate. But this is not a very convincing excuse, and even if it were it would not bring much consolation to our secretary as she waits, abstractedly scrutinizing the toe of her shoe, while we grope for another *cliché*.

BAZOOKAS ON THE MATTERHORN

" 'I can't think what they want *us* here for at all,' said the man with the anti-tank rifle." It was during what we now remember (if indeed we remember it at all) as the phoney war that MR. EVELYN WAUGH conceived these words to have been spoken, in the course of a battalion exercise in the Chobham area, by a member of Mr. Smallwood's platoon. They must have recurred to such readers of *Put Out More Flags* as noticed in these columns a recent dispatch reporting the first ascent of the Matterhorn by a military unit. The unit was the 43rd Company of the Aosta Battalion of the Alpini. The men were roped together in groups of three or four, and besides mortars and machine guns they carried with them bazookas, which are, *mutatis mutandis*, the equivalent of the 1940 anti-tank rifle. In war it is the unexpected that happens; even the most involuntary students of the subject know this. All the same, however versatile, ubiquitous, and omnisubjugant we conceive our potential enemies to be, it is far from easy to visualize a situation in which armour might be deployed against a company of infantry ensconced on the summit of the Matterhorn; and it is correspondingly difficult to believe that the Italian bazooka-men, as they inched their way upwards over the icy slopes, were sustained by any very clear vision of their tactical *raison d'être*.

To carry coals to Newcastle is a task which, though traditionally redundant and until very recently plainly a subject for laughter, does not require of its executants that they should endure, roped together in groups of three or four, extremes of hardship and of peril. To transport short-range anti-tank weapons to the top of the Matterhorn does, on the other hand, involve exceptional rigours and exertions. Viewed objectively, it is an assignment compared with which the carriage of coals to Newcastle appears sagacious and far-sighted. On this view the considerable exploit of the Alpini might seem open to criticism. What was the point, the armchair tacticians will ask, of taking bazookas up the Matterhorn? One of the very few predictions which can be made with confidence about the course of any future conflict is that tanks, however imaginatively handled, will by-pass all mountain peaks over (say) ten or twelve thousand feet above sea-level, and in most cases will by-pass them by a comfortable margin.

Few will quarrel with this forecast, but man is a curious animal, and tends to become curiouser when he assumes the disguise, at once elaborate and thin, of a soldier. In the ranks of the 43rd Company there can have been nobody, however he was armed, who expected ever to go into action on an inaccessible pinnacle 14,771ft. high; nor can there have been anybody who, had he set out to climb the Matterhorn on his own, would not have left all inessentials behind. Yet the soldier in peace-time is like an actor graduating, *via* farce and comedy, for a part —perhaps a leading and redeeming one—in tragedy. He must observe the illogical conventions, study the fripperies, maintain and even revere the *panache* of inconsequence and impracticability. Perhaps Italian bazookas on the Matterhorn are no more ridiculous, and no less admirable, than British bearskins in a heatwave.

NIGHT AND DAY

Though some profess to enjoy rising early in the morning, in most of us there is an innate sluggishness which HARRY LAUDER confirmed so aptly when he sang, " O it's nice to get up in the morning, but it's nicer to lie in bed." A psychiatrist might say that the seed of this sloth is to be found in a reaction to our schooldays when, with the bell booming through our returning consciousness, we realized that another of the happiest days of our life was at hand, a day which, in some instances, had the even more auspicious start (as related in a recent royal autobiography) of being forced to plunge into an unheated swimming bath, in summer or winter.

But, during the hot weather, the most sybaritic bed-worshipper may be tempted, perhaps because it has been too warm to sleep, to experience that glorious freshness of the summer morn which poets and writers have been dinning into his ears for as long as he can remember. He may even be persuaded to rise before that dawn chorus, somewhat muted during this month, of which LORD GREY of FALLODON wrote so sympathetically—" Unfortunately this wonderful opening of the day occurs at an hour when civilized man is either in sleep or suffering from the want of it. In the first case he does not hear the singing ; in the second he is in no mood to enjoy it." As the riser creeps downstairs (for he likes to conceal his sudden insanity) he finds that house and garden have become strangely unreal ; the very strike of the grandfather clock in the hall seems to have a different timbre to its announcement at midnight, while, outside, the impression of a dream world is even stronger, for those familiar borders, trees, or alleyways between the cypresses have all assumed an insubstantiality in the early mists.

Moreover, in the pond there is no sign yet of his favourite gold fin winking in his porphyry font, for he is still sensibly asleep under a lily pad, and the riser begins to feel that he is alone in an unfriendly world.

What shall he do? He had formerly had vague ideas of mowing the lawn, but would not now dare disturb the unnatural morning calm, nor, even more so, his neighbours. He has thoughts of returning to the marital couch whence he has so secretly crept, but such action also has its dangers, and he wonders if he can cook himself some breakfast, the lack of which is causing part of his depression, without dropping something and arousing the household. It is at such a moment that he almost longs for the cosy darkness of the summer night with its scents and stars and the lamps of the house glowing with welcome through the trees—it seems an unfriendly building now in the brittle light of the rising sun. A thrush is tugging at a worm, and for a fleeting moment the riser feels that he has indeed won some virtue as he remembers his childhood precept that "the early bird catches the worm." Unfortunately for him even that statement, like so many of our aphorisms, is open to contradiction, for any angler could tell the early bird that if he became a nightbird a far greater feast of lobs would be awaiting him in the dew of the lawn.

UNDER THE HAMMER

"Pea-fowl. Antique Man Traps. Garden Statuary. . . ." There are some people who, when they notice in the announcement of a sale that such items as the above are included in " the Valuable Contents of the Mansion," cannot resist pursuing the matter a little further, especially if they know the house or the family to whom it belonged. It is not that they wish to purchase all or any of the pea-fowl, nor are they necessarily the sort of people in whose domestic arrangements an antique man trap would supply a long-felt want. It is for almost sentimental reasons that they interest themselves in the sale and decide that, if it is a fine day, they will join the assorted crowd drifting over the unkempt lawns or loitering aimlessly in the great rooms, which retain, in spite of all the intruders, an air of emptiness. The dealers will be there, dapper and keen eyed and double breasted, and there will be curious passers-by—motorists and cyclists drawn through the lodge gates by idle curiosity. The county will be sporadically represented, exchanging reminiscences of children's parties and shooting luncheons at this place and saying, vaguely, that it seems a shame; and here and there, speaking with unwonted sharpness to their grandchildren, but in between these outbursts maintaining a regretful silence, will be neat old people who in a vanished age worked in the stables or the stillroom and can remember the dogs whose small, neglected tombstones—" Gyp. 1899-1908. A Faithful Friend "—cluster under the yew tree by the ha-ha.

It will be, on the whole, rather a sad occasion, filled with something of the same sense of doom and dissolution that attends the felling of a solitary and ancient tree. But there is nothing, in the meanwhile, to prevent us from enjoying the catalogue. Its style, though sedate, is rich. Cassones and torchères, ottomans and fauteuils, tazze and tureens and ramekins, garnitures and purdoniums—we feel ourselves transported to a world of rather exotic opulence; and even when we get, so to speak, to the tail of the team, where the pea-fowl and the man traps are sent in to bat among "miscellaneous odd joinery," "sundry drainpipes," and "a pair of Badminton standards," we are always apt to come across something pretty solid, like "a blacksmith's forge" or "a bronze life-sized draped female garden figure seated on rock base with winged Cupid supporting a basket, 61 inches high." Whether, if we go, we shall buy anything ourselves is doubtful; but as the treasures and the junk are dispersed by the tireless auctioneer to new and not so stately homes, it will be worth watching, for an hour or two, a not unusual phenomenon of our age. We may even, if we hold the right doctrines, enjoy the spectacle.

TWO MEN IN A PUNT

De minimis non curat lex is all very fine, but lawyers, expertly counting their smallest change, are always a fascinating sight to a layman. He follows them as they split the hairs of Commonwealth-shaking issues in the Privy Council with interest no more absorbing than he gives to the subtlety of argument in less exalted courts. Subtlety had a field day, recently, in the pleasant and historic city of Limerick, where two fishermen found themselves charged with behaviour contrary to the Summary Jurisdiction Act of 1908. The story which brought them before the Justice began when they met a sailor and had a few drinks with him. They then embarked on the lovely but tricky waters of the river Shannon, where it is eighteen feet deep, in a small punt which a sergeant, under cross-examination, agreed was unsuitable for such navigation. It was also agreed that the navigators were in less than their best nautical form.

Both were described in court as having been seen from the bank to sway in their little craft. One of them fell on his back and remained in that position with his head hanging out over the side. On being asked by a police sergeant to come into the slip, they ignored him and kept moving downstream. The sergeant then went to St. Michael's Boat Club, the windows of which offered a stalls view of the proceedings, and asked members to take out a rescue vessel. Members told him that they had already appealed to the men to come ashore, but in vain. They now launched what may be described as a river lifeboat, but when they were still some twelve yards from the punt one of the punters fell into the water. Happily a passing motorist who belonged to the Shannon

Rowing Club dived in and held the man's head above the water until help arrived.

Up to this point all seems plain sailing to a layman—so far, that is, as the law is concerned, though the words could hardly be applied to the voyage of the punt. It may have been, as was suggested, that one of the defendants had been trying to give a cigarette to the other before he fell in, but, whatever the details, a conviction for " drunk in charge " looked like a safe bet. True, the Justice himself answered the question, " Who was in charge, sergeant ? " with " No one." He also remarked, " I am thirty years in court and I never heard of anyone being drunk in charge of a boat," and the police superintendent, who prosecuted, agreed that he had never heard of it either. Still, the unusual is not necessarily the legal and it remained for the ingenious solicitor for the defendants to raise a doubt as to how the law could concern itself with this scene witnessed from the banks of the Shannon. The summons, he contended, accused his clients of being in charge of a vehicle, to wit, a boat, and a boat, on his plea, was not a vehicle, and, further, they were not in charge of it. This was a sporting effort to prove that the summons, like the curate's egg, was bad in parts, but the Justice ruled that it could be amended, and amended it was, by the superintendent, to " in possession of an article." As the farseeing draftsman of the Summary Jurisdiction Act of 1908 had included this alternative to vehicle, one of the defendants was sentenced to twenty-one days in gaol and the other fined forty shillings. The suggestion that the gaoled punter might appeal was raised and, in giving the amount of the sureties to meet this eventuality, the Justice said : " He is very lucky that he is not appealing from the next world." Whatever his future he is likely to remember that a punt, like a glass of stout, is an " article " within the meaning of the Act.

SMALL MERCIES

It is quite often, and sometimes with truth, said of a man that he had not an enemy in the world. It is extremely doubtful whether a similar claim has ever been made on behalf of a nation. The more irreproachable a nation's conduct in international affairs, the milder and more pacific the demeanour of its citizens, the more likely it is to excite the cupidity of a powerful neighbour. At the other end of the scale, the more sturdily a nation asserts its intentions to defend its interests and its frontiers the more certain it is to attract the odium of those who regard this attitude as minatory and aggressive. In between these two extremes, the middlepiece nations, whose weakness is not obvious enough to act as a temptation and whose strength is too inconsiderable to constitute a threat, somehow contrive to excite indignation or disapproval by their personal habits, this one being reviled for the laxity of its morals and that one scoffed at for its strait-laced Puritanism.

The British, though in their simple way they take it for granted that they will inspire affection and respect in some of their neighbours, can never quite make out why others take such an extraordinarily poor view of them. Execrated at one time or another by the Spaniards, the French, the Dutch, the Americans, the Chinese, the Germans, and many others, they have come at last to accept with a reasonable degree of fatalism the fact that at any given moment of history some foreigner's blood will be boiling at the mere thought of their existence. In time of war an enemy is, of course, a necessary evil; the thing could not go on without him. In time of peace, when he is not technically an enemy at all, he is merely a great nuisance, and it is by their nuisance value that the average Briton tends to judge the various Powers which in his lifetime have cast themselves for the traditional, but in the long run rather unrewarding, role of his country's enemy.

There can be no doubt that the Russians, who are at present acting this part, give a performance which is in one important respect preferable to that given, not so very long ago, by the Germans. In what we now call a cold war words, which supply the bulk of the ammunition discharged, count for a great deal. No one would accuse the Russians of mincing theirs when they speak (as they continually do) of the misdeeds and shortcomings of the western democracies ; but the repetition of a theme, though it is valuable in propaganda, tends when the propaganda is mainly abusive to produce in the long run an almost soporific effect. Hyenas, Imperialists, war-mongers, lackeys, running dogs—we ought to wince at each impact of these serious accusations. Somehow we do not. Like the murmur of the sea when you hold a shell to your ear, they come to us inexplicably, out of nothing, from a long way away. How different, and how much more of a nuisance, was the technique of the last actor to sustain this role ! The output of MARSHAL STALIN's propaganda machine may be as great, or greater than, the late HERR HITLER's, the tone of his diplomatic communications no less uncompromising, but the effect of it all is rather stereotyped ; and, above all, MARSHAL STALIN does not from time to time deliver, at the top of his voice and generally at the week-end, those turgid and protracted orations which, in HERR HITLER's day, we awaited with so much foreboding and anatomized with so much care. It is unflattering to be called a hyena at frequent intervals ; but most of us can remember worse evils of this kind.

M—2

WESTERN APPROACHES

What should they know of England who only England know? American visitors arriving for the first time might well, before they make their landfall, answer KIPLING'S question with "any number of quaint things." The thoughtful British Travel and Holidays Association vies with the steamship companies to put our guests into the picture long before they come in sight of Land's End. A fascinating little library of pamphlets is to be had for the asking on board, and a British subject who has the good luck to study them in the company of American fellow-passengers is made ashamed of his ignorance. He learns, as he sits in his deck-chair, that the people of the West Midlands talk a local dialect and look upon London as being as remote as Babylon and perhaps as wicked. A lonely pedestrian in the Lowlands of Scotland will, he is warned, run a danger of getting panic-stricken as the long shadows from the hills creep stealthily across the moors.

The Highlands sound no less strange, for there is more magic in them than anywhere else on earth, but the true heart of Scotland is neither Highland nor Lowland. It is to be sought in the centre—not only geographically and economically but also from the all-important viewpoint of history. Browsing over this general information his attention is distracted from time to time by points of detail. Five miles from Blackburn JAMES I knighted a loin of beef and thereby created the word sirloin. Yorkshire is, without doubt, the most versatile of English counties, and it contains as many acres as there are letters in the Bible. Gloomily contemplating that he will not be able to indulge in a Continental holiday this summer, he is shown that his native island is a hive of activities which any curious traveller should be sorry to miss. A ship docking to-day (July 19) arrives just too late for the old custom of Lighting the Baal Fire at Whalton, for Walking Day at Warrington, and for the Callants Festival at Jedburgh. Regret for these missed chances may be forgotten in contemplation of events still ahead. The Common Riding at Langholm, the Abbots Bromley Horn Dance, the Ould Lammas Fair at Ballycastle, the " Knighthood of Old Green " bowls at Southampton, and the Hythe Venetian Fête are still to come. For amateurs of Well Dressings there is a positive orgy of fixtures in Derbyshire, and for those who prefer Rushbearing the ceremony can be witnessed at least twice in the Lakes. There is yet time to see the contest for the " Ancient Scorton Arrow " at Harrogate.

A snake lurks in this old-world Eden, and the British subject is made aware of it when he sees his American companions scratching their heads over a leaflet called " Britain's Money." This gives illustrations of our confusing coinage, and the British heart bleeds for the strangers as they point at the two different brands of threepenny bit and ask one another why if a penny equals one cent, one shilling (equals twelve pence) is fourteen cents and half a crown (two and a half shillings) thirty-five cents. In puzzled tones they speculate about the mysterious crown or five-shilling piece, which is not shown in the pictures but may, they fear, turn up in their change, and they cannot understand why many prices should be expressed in guineas, although, as they are told, there is no paper or coin of this denomination. Perplexity grows when explorers, who have seen Ireland first and joined the ship at Cobh, display a handful of coins decorated with pigs and hens and horses. Will these, the question is raised, be accepted in Britain ? and the answer has to be " No," although, by way of another injustice, British coins circulate without let or hindrance in Ireland. Such conundrums are dismissed as a kindly captain steers close to the Cornish cliffs and the loudspeaker draws attention to Lizard Head. Then a new mystery arises. Why, comes the challenge to the Britisher, do you folk talk about the white cliffs of England? Enviable are these pilgrims who see Cornwall and Kent alike as virgin soil! Britain is a lovely island and how lovely, its sons and daughters may reflect, if they could see the granite and the chalk coastlines and the green hinterland for the first time.

THE GENTLEMAN AND HIS LIBRARY

As an architectural entity the library has ceased to be a normal feature of most modern households. Until fairly recently every gentleman's residence was provided with a room lined with well-stocked bookshelves. A small step-ladder, enabling the more agile type of gentleman to reach the uppermost shelves, leant in a corner; and more often than not, though for no very good reason, there were one or two busts about. In this room the gentleman, if able, read; slept after luncheon on Sundays; wrote letters; interviewed blackmailers and the vicar; practised his speech for the flower show; cut his son off with a shilling; and—in many cases—was foully and mysteriously done to death. Unless the house belonged to some kind of savant, the library was normally in intermittent rather than continuous use; but, as has been indicated, it was the *locus classicus* of many interesting activities for which modern domestic architecture has so far failed to evolve a satisfactory alternative setting—and it was, of course, an extraordinarily handy place for keeping books in.

It is perhaps this purely functional aspect of the library's usefulness that the modern householder misses most. In the old days, if the library was being redecorated, a gentleman could always interview blackmailers in the billiard room; and even in the most cramped and least sound-proof modern dwelling there is generally somewhere where confidential transactions of this nature can be carried out. Blackmailers, in any case, are relatively infrequent visitors to even the worst regulated households, and, having come, they go away again. Books are not like this. However undiscriminating our taste in literature, however little leisure life allows us for reading, the number of books in our house or flat tends to increase steadily year by year. The wastage due to unscrupulous visitors or uncontrollable puppies is too trivial to offset the steady though random increment of reading matter. Apart from our own voluntary and involuntary acquisitions (prominent among the latter being the entire literary output of a prolific female cousin, from whom we receive every Christmas her latest production), our children's supposed needs add to the pressure on our limited shelf-space. Though alarmingly slow in learning to read, they are now making up for lost time. They would not put their books away even if there were anywhere to put them, and the premises are ankle-deep in fairy-stories, space-fiction and books about unnaturally well behaved ponies.

There are obvious and simple remedies for this state of affairs, and in the more methodical type of household they are periodically put into effect. The bookshelves are purged and rearranged, the redundant volumes are sent off to some deserving institute which can readily find a use for them, and order and symmetry are restored. But there are people who for one reason or another never quite get around to doing this. They scratch, sometimes, at the surface of the job, pulling out a volume here and a volume there. The book on economics which they never even began, the long novel about the American Civil War which they never finished, a technical work dealing with silage, the autobiography of a bore—these and others, they decide, can go. Can go? No doubt. But do they go? They go, perhaps, as far as the hall, where they stand for weeks in an untidy pile. Space-fiction and treatises on the care of rabbits infiltrate into the gaps where they once stood, and when in the end some discerning benefactor presents the household with a new book-case the outcasts are reprieved and fall in once more, in their totally unreadable ranks, upon the shelves. There is really a great deal to be said for the old-fashioned library, even if it was apt to harbour the odd assassin.

END OF TERM GROUP

The sight of small boys in red, green, or blue caps carrying cricket bats is an entirely commonplace one at every railway station ; but in their luggage, for which harassed mothers are hunting, they often carry something which Sherlock Holmes would have called a little *recherché*. In a future so dim and far away as to be inconceivable they will be very sorry to have lost it. This is the photographic group. Once this was of the whole school taken at the end of the summer term, with the head master beaming imperially in the middle ; the assistant masters gathered round him like NAPOLEON'S marshals ; on either side the matron and a master's wife or two and even a privileged little girl, a production of one of them. Then there were the boys, four rows of them ; the smallest on the grass symmetrically cross-legged, like so many Rugby half-backs ; the largest scattered in the central seats of the mighty and the other two standing behind. Nowadays the group may sometimes be only of a cricket team, but all in it are, still, like the young oysters who so unwisely came hurrying to the treat.

> Their coats were brushed, their faces washed,
> Their shoes were clean and neat.

Except that in the modern and sensible fashion they have no coats, but are in shirt sleeves. About them one and all is an appearance of smiling virtue, a *Non Angli sed Angeli* air. Here, muses the grown-up, are the elements of a mild devilry in the most deceptive repose. As he is piloted round the group by its owner, he learns the most astonishing legends that remind him of his own private school days. " That," he is told, " is Mr. X. He's seven feet high." A gentle protest evokes the reply, " Well, anyway, he's a lot taller than you." "That's Mr. Y. I don't like him" seems to suggest ill-disciplined confidence better left unspoken. It is safer to pass on to the owner's "gang" in which each initiate is known by the name of an animal—elephant, cart-horse, and so on down to the newest and humblest gangster, the ant.

Unless that grown-up is of truly callous fibre such pictures will arouse in him almost unbearable yearnings. He must at one time have possessed many such groups, and where are they now? It can only be assumed that time, the devourer of all things, has made a meal of them. There may, indeed, be left just one photograph which turns up periodically as did the old school list of J.K.S.

> In a wild moraine of forgotten books
> On the glacier of years gone by.

At the moment it is not to be found, but some day it will certainly reappear, proudly showing the eleven in their caps of red and white stripes, their shirts of rather starchy canvas (the eleven's exclusive prerogative), and their ties of white silk that were likewise part of that full dress uniform. It is very beautiful but where, alas! are all its companions that might have been? It is the duty of parents to keep these pictures safe till their owners are old enough to take them over. There are photographs such as those taken at public dinners by an insinuating gentleman with a flashlight which can surely tempt very few; but these old school groups are in a different category. They are one with the tin soldiers and stamp albums of days gone by. Their precious quality is recognized only when it is too late.

GOOD EGGS

Irony, never in these days more than round the corner, if as far, has just issued news of an enormous incubator, capable of handling 357,000 eggs. It is not the fault of the hens that there is an egg shortage, for they are now trained to deliver their goods with the professional precision of an Olympic sprinter. Belated travellers in the countryside may see in the small hours the electric glow of the up-to-date, day-and-night arenas, specially designed for non-stop egg-laying. Modern hens may look back on the old amateurs of the farmyard with the tolerant pity of a lady who can cover a hundred yards in round about eleven seconds contemplating the mincing and leisurely progress of her grandmother. Whether there is such a creature as a modern hen is what owners (or hosts) of a mere handful of hens may doubt. Birds, as all the best ornithologists believe, are pretty automatic affairs, rather nearer to a plant than to a human being in their reactions. Give them a balanced diet and so forth and they will lay away like mad or, at any rate, like cogs in a factory process. Judging by results this is, perhaps, true, but—as anyone who has been on friendly terms with hens must ask—do they like it?

Left to themselves in the comparative freedom of a small man's run, they quickly develop distinct personalities. One will be found with exasperating regularity wandering audibly at large among the flower beds and she will continue to find ways and means of truancy whatever barricades are raised against her. Another will, however sternly she is watched, never fail to emerge clucking triumphantly after having hidden her egg beyond the nettles in the most inaccessible corner of the "estate." Although the murmuring, muted chorus, as the inmates are shut up for the night, is a combined effort, cannot individual voices be detected? The house is dark and unequipped with constant temperature and humidity controls. Only the "fug" of those within saves it from being infernally cold in winter, and in July it must be stuffy. The owner who is sure that no criticism of his housing plans is being uttered, as he makes good against a vixen with cubs to feed, has never known a hen. Still less has he known a duck. There is a bird that is fairly bursting with idiosyncrasies. She will, if she is given the chance, start sitting for the first time in her life at the age of ten, and the elderly duck who, growing bored with the monotony of sex, chooses to turn, so far as appearances go, into a dashing young drake is no freak of the biologists. She appears of her own accord on the edge of the least scientifically watched pond and very gallant she looks in borrowed plumes.

Can it be that these wayward birds really do adapt themselves happily to the regimented way of living? A hen is unquestionably proud of having laid an egg.

> Like Royalty, she goes her way,
> Laying foundations every day,
> Though not for Public Buildings, yet
> For custard, cake and omelette.

The egg, she surely and truly knows, is mightier than the pen. She admits that the proverbs are right in denying that eggs can be shaved or unscrambled, but who on earth would want to perform such footling acts? That one egg is exactly like another she will find impossible to accept. For a craftswoman, each accomplished performance comes fresh, and as she tells the world that she has done it again her notes are as infectiously gay as any known to DR. KOCH himself. "Mine honest friend," says the King in *The Winter's Tale*, "will you take eggs for money?" The hen says the same, adding "but there is a delight in laying that no money can buy "—and every duck, paddling on the water, quacks approval. It was a Frenchman who claimed that his countrymen had 685 ways of cooking eggs. For a hen there are as many ways of laying them—but how many can be practised when it has all been narrowed to an industrial exercise?

TO SANDRINGHAM

CHRISTMAS: 1951

The spirit of the PRINCE CONSORT may well smile at this season on the family party in the home which, with characteristically far sighted wisdom, he arranged for his eldest son to acquire. Sandringham is new among royal palaces, but for its owners it echoes pleasantly with memories of happy childhood, and, for their subjects, it has won a specially warm corner in hearts all over the Commonwealth. Other palaces have more resounding histories and are associated with greater matters of state, but none is more fragrant with the sweet sanctities of family life than is Sandringham. The generations that have met there in recent years have come with added vividness into the lives of other families, united or scattered across the Commonwealth, because of the KING's broadcast. To-morrow, at three o'clock, the KING's voice (this time recorded beforehand as a safeguard after the strain put upon HIS MAJESTY by the grave illness through which he has so gallantly come) will cast a never-failing spell over the revelry of his people at home and oversea. Ever since the KING's father began this memorable series, broadcasting may be said to have strengthened the rays of limelight playing upon a Sandringham Christmas, but this, for all its value and charm, is incidental. The central theme would be the same if wireless had never been invented. It is of kinsmen and kinswomen, grandparents, parents, and children assembled under their own roof to keep the Christian feast.

The hold of Sandringham on British affection is now so sure and so traditional that the reflexion may seem surprising that very old folk still alive can remember the interest which their elders took in the acquisition of this country seat for EDWARD VII, when he was Prince of Wales and still a bachelor. His father directed that a large part of the accumulated revenues of the Duchy of Cornwall should be set aside for the purchase of a demesne of about 7,000 acres of which SPENCER COWPER, an owner of old county standing, was the absentee landlord. This shooting box—it was then little more—in Norfolk had a rent roll of some £7,000 a year, but large sums had to be spent under the supervision of the PRINCE, who entered zestfully into the plans for putting the property into good order. Within a year of his first trial of his new home, the PRINCE had married, and, from then onwards, Sandringham shared with Marlborough House the loyalty of the royal couple. KING GEORGE V learnt to love it as a child and he brought up his own children to feel happy, as he did, in those quiet East Anglian surroundings.

To-day the two great-great-great-grandchildren of the PRINCE CONSORT, still young enough to be taking their first soundings in life and to be forming those first impressions of surroundings that will remain deep in their consciousness so long as they live, are spending Christmas at Sandringham. Regard for palaces, as for more humble homes, is not invariably handed down from parents to children. Osborne, beloved by QUEEN VICTORIA, was disposed of with understandable lack of regret after her death. Even her ties with Balmoral have from time to time been relaxed by her descendants. Sandringham, as is the way with homes in which children have been happy, has gone from strength to strength. For the KING, to-morrow, there will be past memories as well as present laughter to make him know that he is at home and has the greatest of all good fortunes at Christmas, to be there with those nearest and dearest to him. His subjects, in company and in loneliness, in Britain and far away, when they raise their glasses, will look to Sandringham.